To Norman —

You are a

bright light! Let

it shine ~ ~ ~

Warm regards,

Linda LeClaire

Feb. 2005

ALSO BY LINDA LECLAIRE

Book
The Whole Kid Peace Activity Book:
Promoting Self-Esteem, Preventing Conflict
(by Peggy Henrikson and Lorraine O. Moore, Ph.D.,
with Linda LeClaire and Pamela S. Welter)

Audiotapes
The Confidence Factor
Tennis/Singles Play
Basketball
Baseball
Golf

Audiotapes with Dr. Bryce Young
Quantum Doubles
From Anger to Athletic Excellence
Play • Recover • Prepare

(See last page to order.)

Yes, God speaks to women too!

A message of... health, healing, and hope

Linda LeClaire

Minneapolis • Visual • Eyes • 1998

Editing/cover design: Lisa LeClaire, Minneapolis
Copy-editing/text design: E. B. Green Editorial, St. Paul
Indexing: Stina Enterprises/Patricia Harpole, St. Paul
Printing: Sexton Printing, Inc., St. Paul
Binding: Muscle Bound Bindery, Minneapolis

Library of Congress Catalog Card Number: 98-61249
ISBN: 0-9665696-0-1
Manufactured in the United States of America
10 9 8 7 6 5 4 3 2 1

With love and gratitude to

my Mom, Lorene Welter, who taught me
what love looks like, and

my Dad, Ray Welter, who taught me
what truth looks like

. . . in everyday moments

Contents

Preface

"Yes, Linda! God speaks to women, too!"

So began my conversations with God. How do I know it was God? God told me so.

Since the conversations began, I have felt my own energy shift. My awareness has been heightened. My thinking is clearer. My life is fuller. I appreciate every day. I am different.

This is not an ordinary book. After all, it is a conversation with God. I was intrigued by these conversations. I asked the questions; God answered. I wrote only when the energy was with me. Sometimes I wrote for hours. Other times, minutes. It didn't matter where we were, sometimes even in the middle of a thought, when it was time to stop. If the energy was gone, it was gone. There was no more writing that day.

I tried for several years to write this book. I had been hearing these messages for a long time and wanted to share them. When I was working with someone on the phone or in my office, it was easy. But when I tried to write the words, they seemed flat and lifeless—until that autumn day when God took over.

Sometimes my own life came up. I wouldn't want to write about it, but before I knew what was happening, we were talking about it. When I went into doubt, that became the topic of the day. It was very natural, this conversation with God. And, I suspect, not really so unusual. I have always talked to God. Haven't you? I just started listening better—hearing, finally. Every time I wrote something I felt better about myself and my body. The writing was a healing for me.

This is an instruction manual, a basic guide to living in a body, peacefully. Though the ideas are simple and clear, I find myself returning to them again and again, discovering deeper meaning with each new reading. That the message is love is obvious. I have been using love more in my life. It works, much better than fear ever did.

I use these instructions with my clients. It doesn't matter whether they are bronco riders or golfers, figure skaters or bull riders, hockey or basketball players, tennis or baseball players. The instructions work with all sports. I work with clients wanting to lose weight. It works with them. I work with clients afraid to make a phone call, to give speeches, or just to get through the day. It works with them. I work with clients traumatized by abuse. It works with them, too. The more I work with other people, the easier it is for me to live by this philosophy. The instructions are clear and simple, yet powerful.

As you read, stay with the questions. Allow the answers to come from God. To make it easier to read, I have done some editing—not that it's easy to edit God. You will first read an overview of the body and how it works, then a description of the four main components of the body—the physical, mental, emotional, and spiritual. These descriptions include the needs as well as the functions of each component. Then we move

Preface

into more detail, talking about our inner tools. Doubt and fear come in. We talk about emotions and feelings—heart energy. We talk about the body as a system of energy and information, about how fear blocks our energy and love keeps our energy flowing freely. We talk about death. That was hard for me, at first. God helped, and soon I felt better about death, too. I am no longer afraid of it. My work with clients is woven through our conversations. The names are not real, but the stories are.

Don't let the title fool you. This is a book for all people—men and women—though the title does seem to have its own message. We are all loved and honored in the eyes of God. It doesn't matter whether you believe in God, Goddess, or Higher Power. What is important is that this information work for you. I know it works for me. If it does work for you, tell your friends about it. Help me spread the word.

May you always express peace and love while in your precious body.

LINDA LeCLAIRE
Summer 1998

Acknowledgments

I am grateful to so many people who have been loving and supportive of my work. You may not even know how much you have helped me, but I do.

First of all, of course, my gratitude and appreciation to my coauthor—God—for the inspiration that kept me going and the love that fills me.

I feel more gratitude and pleasure than I can express for the opportunity to have worked with my personal editor, cover designer, and stepdaughter, Lisa LeClaire. Her enthusiasm and courage to edit not only my words, but God's as well, is more than appreciated. I will never be able to thank her enough for expressing her love and unending creativity in the design of the beautiful cover for this book.

Boundless love and gratitude to my son, Josh LeClaire, for being able to express his love and respect for me and our unusual lifestyle. His smile always brightens my day.

The moon and stars to my best friend, writer and poet Pamela S. Welter, for all the hours she has listened to me discuss my philosophy, questioning and interviewing me until I

Acknowledgments

could express clearly what is in my heart and soul. And most of all for caring enough to want to know me.

A rose to my Mom, Lorene Welter, for her support in spreading the word of my book to everyone she knows, including strangers on airplanes!

Gratitude to my whole family, especially to my brothers, Dale Welter, Denny Welter and Larry Welter, for keeping me in balance with their male perspectives and for their love and support of my work. And to my sisters, Beverly Tschimperle and Carol Lenzen, for their female perspective as well as for their love and support.

Much gratitude to my editor, Ellen B. Green. Her patience with my inexperience with the final editing process along with her expertise made the last stages of publishing an exciting and joyful experience.

Thanks to Patricia Harpole for creating an index that makes sense.

Thank you to my dear friend Lorraine Moore for reading my first draft and giving suggestions that helped and encouraged me.

Blessings to my precious friend Valerie Williams, whose loving attention to detail got my business up and running.

Blessings to Ann and Lee LeClaire for their continued love and support.

Gratitude to Peter Durand of DuraLogic, Inc., a computer genius who patiently and generously taught me how to use my new computer.

Special thanks to my soul companions, Gail and Bill Roddy for long talks, love, and encouragement. Bill saved me many times when my computer was challenging me. Gail's own book has been an inspiration to me.

Pleasant soul travels to Fred Alan Wolf for encouraging me to write this book long before I knew it was in me.

Rainbows to Michael and Denise Young for their love and encouragement.

Gratitude to Steve Wilkinson, who has been with me from the beginning in my endeavors to express my philosophy and who has taught me so much through his work with Tennis and Life Camps.

Thank you to my dear friend and fellow author Peggy Henrickson for her love and support.

Blessings to my soul sister, Leah Young, who has been living this philosophy for ninety-two years, for reading my first draft with such enthusiasm and encouragement.

Hugs and hearts to Sarah Glover, whose natural expression of love and joy refreshes my spirit more times than she'll ever know. She is an angel in my life as well as in my son's.

Gratitude to Kathy Stoddart at Mail Boxes Etc., for her kind and generous help with my copying needs.

Gratitude to my wise business friend, Beth Brille, for feedback and encouragement on my first draft.

Magical mystical travels to Ken and Ann Nordboe for taking the time to read my first draft and giving me encouragement and support.

Hearts and flowers to Marnie and Carl Hensel for reading the first draft and always encouraging and supporting me in my work.

Eagles to Michele Redman not only for reading my first draft but also for applying its philosophy on the golf course.

Thank you to Coach Martin Novak and to Tracy Novak for their support and enthusiasm for my work.

Acknowledgments

Much appreciation to Coach Dana Peterson for her love and support.

My gratitude to all my clients who so openly shared their stories with me. A special thanks to the teams and individual athletes who have raised their level of performance by following these instructions, learning to play and compete with their hearts and souls.

Honors to the students of my eighteen years of teaching in Wayzata. They, of course, have played a huge role in my growth and evolution. The encouragement and support they gave upon my decision to leave one kind of teaching for another are still with me.

Aces to Tarah Elkins, Jennifer Hayes, Jana Hrdinova, Alice Rangsithienchai, Nora Sauska, Kim Simonsen, Jenni Svehla, Helen Wang, Tammy Wang, Meghan Donley, and Stephany LaBathe, who are all so special and unique that they keep me motivated to discovering new ways of teaching this philosophy. They hold a special place in my heart.

And last, but certainly not least, a grand and heartfelt toast to my special friend and loving partner Bryce Young, for reading my first draft, helping with the editing, listening to my stories, and especially for expressing in many, many ways his love and belief in me and my work.

—LINDA LECLAIRE

Introduction

God: **Yes, Linda! God speaks to women, too!**

Linda: Who are you? What did you say?

God: I am God. And I said that I speak to women, too!

Linda: What are you talking about? If you are God, why are you talking to me? What is this all about?

God: You have asked me to speak to you. You have asked me to speak to a woman. You seem to think that men have misunderstood me.

Linda: Well, that's for sure. God would never say some of the things men seem to think God has said.

God: And what things are you referring to?

Linda: Oh, you know! "Women are inferior to men." "Men are the masters of women." Things like that. Men don't respect women. They think they are better than women. More worthy! I don't even want to talk about it.

God: And are all men like this?

Linda: No, of course not! But I . . . who are you anyway?

God: God.

Linda: If you are God, why are you talking to me?

God: Because you have asked me. You have asked me to tell you how you can be of service. You have offered to help. I am here to tell you.

Linda: How?

God: How can you be of service?

Linda: Yes!

God: By being yourself. By expressing in every moment who you are.

Linda: That's where we have trouble, isn't it? We don't even know who we are. But in asking how I can be of service, I meant "How can I help others?"

God: By knowing yourself. Only then can you really be of help. If you don't know who you are, how can you possibly teach others to know themselves? That is the essence of what you do. You, Linda, are a teacher. You always have been. It is your mission. It is time for you to teach what you know best.

Linda: What is that? What do you mean?

God: You already are doing it. You often say that what you are doing now is the easiest thing you've ever done. That it feels like you have been preparing to do self-improvement teaching your whole life. And so you have. Your life experiences have prepared you well.

Linda: Please, be clearer.

God: You are teaching people how to know themselves. You are teaching people how to know love. How to be their highest selves, no matter what situation they are in. You are doing it through sport. You are doing it through your work with the body. You are doing it through your work with the inner tools. You are doing it through your work with hypnosis. You are doing it through your work with energy—especially with energy. You are doing it through your work with fear. Have you not noticed the interest that people show in what you say about fear? You have been a good student. You have been willing to study fear as well as love. It is now time for you to share what you have discovered on a larger scale.

Linda: A larger scale?

God: Yes. You have said that you are ready. Are you not?

Linda: Yes, I am, though I'm not sure what "larger scale" means. You are making more out of what I am doing than I deserve. It is not even work to me.

God: And yet it is work. But I never said that work was not meant to be your joy as well! You say that only because you are doing what is truly your mission. It is meant to be easy. To be joyful. Even to be blissful.

Linda: Well, that is true. I do feel great when I am working. It has never felt like this when I have done any other work. It is the best feeling in the world. Are you really God?

God: Yes, I am.

Linda: Please then, keep talking. I have a million questions.

God: I know. I am here to answer them. You have asked for the instruction manual for living in a body. That is what I am giving to you, now.

Linda: Now? How?

God: In this book you've been talking about writing for the last couple of years. Don't you think it is about time to begin writing?

Linda: Yes, but every time I start to write, it just doesn't sound right.

God: It will now. You and I are going to do it together. I know you said you wanted to do it alone . . .

Linda: Oh, no, that's okay! I'd love to co-author a book with You. I want the world to know that God speaks to women, too!

God: And so it shall! This is going to be quite fun!

Linda: God is talking to me! I can hardly find the keys, my fingers are moving so fast.

God: Get ready, it's time to do some work. People need to know more about the body system they have chosen to inhabit. They need to know how to be at peace in their bodies. I want you to tell them how to do it.

Linda: Now, that would be great! Many people are at war with their bodies, which causes a lot of pain and suffering.

God: I am going to tell you what your body needs in order for you to be at peace in it. Not only at peace but successful, too, at whatever you really, truly, desire to do. I want you to follow my instructions. Take my word for it, do it, and then decide for yourself! That is how you find out my message really works.

Linda: Oh, boy, that is going to get me in trouble. People will think this is all my idea.

God: And so it is. What difference does it make, anyway?

Linda: It makes a lot of difference. If it is coming from God, people will listen. If it is coming from me, well, that's a different story! What do I know?

God: Don't be so sure. Have I not spoken before through others? Don't many of you believe the Bible comes from me? Yet people do not always heed those words. No, no, Linda. People will listen to you. Much of what you write will be from your experience.

Linda: I thought we were going to write this together. That You were going to be telling me what to say.

Introduction

God: Linda, you get to say whatever you want to say. You and I will have a conversation. You will start out by asking me your questions. We will go from there and see where we arrive. I am going to give you instructions on how to live in a physical body. But I want this to be a dialogue between you and me. Linda, what is your intent in writing this book?

Linda: To teach people how to live peacefully in their bodies. And to teach people how to get their bodies to do what they want them to do. I work with athletes who want to know how to perform or compete at higher and higher levels. Also people who are overweight, sick, and just not happy in their bodies! I want to help them heal too.

God: You want to help anyone who is in a body. Is that right?

Linda: Yes! But You make it sound so grandiose!

God: It is grand! All service is grand, is it not?

Linda: Yes, I see what You mean. You know what?

God: What?

Linda: I like talking to You like this. God does speak to women! I'll do it! I'll write a book, a book about living in a body with You.

God: Perfect!

Linda: What I meant to say was, "I'll write a book with You, about living in a body."

God: That too! You know, Linda, it does take courage for a woman to write that she is co-authoring a book with God. It has not been easy in the past for women who have spoken my mind. You can change that.

Linda: You mean I can help change that?

God: Linda, there you go, changing my words.

Linda: What do You mean?

God: I said, "You can change that," not "You can help change that."

Linda: Oh, well, I thought it would be easier for people to accept, if I said "help."

God: Didn't you say that you didn't like it when men changed what I had said and put it in their own words?

Linda: Yes, but I wasn't putting anyone down by doing that.

God: You were putting yourself down.

Linda: But . . .

God: No, Linda. I want you to write my words as I give them to you. I know what I am saying.

Linda: I didn't mean to imply that You didn't. I am not always sure whether I am hearing You correctly. Maybe I am making mistakes, just as I feel men have in writing Your word. I don't want to do that. I want to be accurate.

God: Never fear, my dear. People will know when I speak. They will feel the truth of it in their bodies. At their core. What they do not hear as truth, they will not use. It is as simple as that.

Linda: Why me?

God: You asked! Do you want the job?

Linda: Yes, of course!

God: Then it is yours. Shall we begin?

Linda: Yes!

God: You have listened well, my child. Fear not, for this is a journey of love, as well as a journey into the workings of the body.

1

The Journey Begins

L. God?

G. Yes?

L. Where do I begin? I don't know what to ask. Help!

G. Begin with a question. It is no different from before. I have always been with you.

L. Have we really begun?

G. Yes!

L. Are you really God, or am I just making this up?

G. Yes.

L. Yes, you are God, or yes I am making it up?

G. Yes, I am God. And I am making it up. I made up the whole universe! I can certainly make this up.

L. I didn't know how You would sound, but this doesn't sound very godlike. I feel like I am talking to some wiseacre.

G. I have been accused of that.

L. That brings me to my friend Pam's question. Are You male or female?

G. You already know the answer to that question. You all do. I am female. I am male. I am neither. I am.

L. Well, I have to tell You that I don't think that answer will satisfy Pam.

G. I'll take care of Pam. Don't worry.

L. What do You mean, "I'll take care of Pam?"

G. You've been watching too many movies. I'll take care of Pam, just as I take care of all my children. Now let's get on with your questions. Remember, this is an instruction manual about how to live in your body.

L. Okay! I have a question. What is the most important thing we can do to keep our bodies healthy?

G. That sounds like another question from Pam!

L. It is!

G. It is a good question. Your body loves to move. Keep moving your body. Exercise. Walk. Use it or lose it! It's easy. And yes, it is supposed to be fun! I don't know where all those ideas about pain and sacrifice came from. They didn't come from me.

L. Do we have to be athletes to have healthy, strong bodies?

G. Everyone's physical body is meant to be that of an athlete. You are all athletes. You don't have to play a sport to be an athlete. Your physical body can do much more than you allow it to do. You place so many limits on it that your body doesn't know what to do.

Your body needs clear instructions. It is a living, breathing, conscious body of energy and information. All that you need is within you. Listen to your body. It is telling you what it needs.

L. That is harder to do than it sounds. I have so many questions. But now I am having trouble thinking of them. Why can't I form them?

G. It's not your questions that block you. It's your answers. Clear your mind of your answers. Come to me with an open mind, a beginner's mind. Allow the answers to come from me. That is what holds people back. They already have decided what the answer is. Or they don't like the answer, and so they say, "I don't know what to do. Everything is so hard for me." They make up excuse after excuse for being miserable. Life is not about being miserable. Life is about love.

Live your life in love, and you'll find the excuses getting fewer and fewer. You'll find your life more and more in tune with who you are. Who you truly are. You have been right all along, Linda. Love is the answer. That is all you need to know. It is simple.

L. Yes, but when we get in these bodies, it is as if we forget that. Why is that?

G. It is part of the game of life. Life in a body! The rules in a body seem to be different, but they're not. It's still about love. You are learning about love. Know that you are love. To experience more of yourself, to go deeper into who you are, you have chosen to experience love through life in a body.

In a body you get to go deeper into the depths of love. Love is splendid! Love is all powerful. You are all-powerful. Even in a body. You are still love. The body is made to thrive in love.

Your assignment is to learn how to access love in every moment of your life in the body. In every circumstance. In every experience.

It has been something of a secret for a long time, and now that the secret is finally out, you have a hard time believing it. You have made it so hard on yourself that you can't believe it is so simple.

L. That's for sure. We need help. We keep getting lost. Stuck in places we don't want to be anymore. The way the body is meant to function seems to hold the key to the way out of our limitations. Let's get back to that.

G. Yes, this is an instruction manual. So, let's start at the beginning. There are four basic parts to the body:

Your body has a physical, a mental, an emotional, and a spiritual component.

Take care of each of these and you will have a very happy and peace-filled body.

L. Which is the most important part?

G. They are all important. Even if one part is not nurtured, it will affect the health of the entire system. They are interdependent.

Yet I can tell you that the spiritual body is the driving force behind the whole system. Your spirit is what inspires you.

10

When your spirit is healthy and strong, you know who you are and what your mission is. You are here for a reason, you know. Each of you is part of the game plan!

It is this sense of mission, this knowing why you are here that gives you strength and courage to keep going. It is also the part of you that keeps you on your path. It is your guiding compass, keeping you going in the right direction. It is through your spiritual body that you hear me. That you experience me.

L. Could you give us an overview of the body and the four components, first?

G. Sure! Then I'll fill in the details for each part. As I was saying earlier, the spiritual body is the driving force. It fuels the entire system. It keeps it going.

Then you have the mental body. It triggers the emotional body. And the emotional body triggers the physical body. That is the usual order. The spiritual body drives the whole system. The mental body gets it going by triggering the emotional body, which then gets the physical body moving.

You can reverse the order, but it works best in this order. It is the easiest to control when you do it in this order. The mind goes a little crazy when something goes on before it has knowledge of it. It'll survive. But it'll make you a bit uncomfortable until it has figured out what is going on. So I suggest you do it in the order it was intended. But variety is the spice of life! Mix it up once in a while.

L. Let me see if I understand the process. The spiritual body fuels my whole system. The mental body sends a message to the emotional body. The emotional body responds to the message, and it sends a message to the physical body. It sounds to me like the mental body is the controlling force. Is that right?

G. Yes and no. Remember that they all are interdependent. A thought without an emotion is lifeless and will have no energy or power to activate the physical body to any form of action. The mind needs the heart. The heart needs the mind.

L. And the spiritual body keeps it going!

G. That's right. Now you're getting it. Think of your body as this incredible moving machine. Only it isn't a machine. It is alive and conscious. It helps to see your body as something you have, rather than as something you are.

You have a body. You are not your body.

L. Is this where the spiritual body comes in?

G. Not exactly. The spiritual body is a part of your individual physical body. I am talking about the soul here. You are a soul in a body. You are your soul, not your body. As soul you live forever, as body you have chosen a limited amount of time for your body to live. Your soul is in charge. Yes, you hear your soul's voice through your spiritual body. That's why it is so important to give your spirit the nourishment it needs. You won't be able to hear the quiet voice of the soul if your spirit is weakened by lack of nourishment. Or if your mind is cluttered with garbage thoughts and thought patterns.

L. This is so interesting! Go on, please!

G. Each body has a "fuel tank." For the body to run efficiently and at top speed, the "fuel tank" of each body has to be full. It will run at lower levels with less fuel but not at its best. If one of the tanks is low or out of fuel, the other bodies will take over. This puts these bodies in stress, overworking them. For short periods of time, it's not a problem.

Over the long run, however, the stress and overdrive speed will cause dis-ease in the physical body, dis-content in the emotional body, distress in the mental body, or depression in the spiritual body.

It's easy. Keep all the "tanks" full, and you will have a happy, peaceful, strong body.

L. What can we learn from athletes and sport?

G. Everyone has a body that is meant for them. A body in which they can live their mission. They have the body that is right for them. Sport has a mission, too. Everything exists for a reason. Sport is meant to teach you about life. It is one way you can learn about yourself and life's challenges in a safe and joyful way. In fact, sport is like a trial run at life. It gives you an opportunity to learn how to use your inner tools. Athletes demonstrate these tools to you.

L. What do you mean by tools?

G. You have within you different forms of energy that help you to do anything you want to do. We are going to call these different energies "tools" because you already have an understanding of the word. You use outer tools to help you create objects in the physical world—like buildings, gardens, vehicles, and so forth. You use inner tools to help you create the life you desire. These tools include anything from fear and doubt to confidence and belief.

L. This definitely sounds like we are going to have a fun journey.

Highlights

1. All that you need is within you.

2. The body needs clear instructions.

3. Exercise is vital for a healthy body.

4. The body has a physical, mental, emotional and spiritual component.

5. Each part must be taken care of.

6. In your essential state, you are love.

7. The spiritual body is the driving force.

8. You have a body. You are not your body.

9. Sport is like a trial run at life.

10. There are both outer and inner tools available to you.

2

The Spiritual Body

G. When you read something that touches you deep inside, hits a cord inside of you, sends goose bumps over your whole body, makes you want to be more of who you are, you are experiencing your spiritual body. It could be through music, nature, art, and even a sports event. Why do you think you are working with so many athletes?

Your spirit needs inspiration, love, and a sense of mission!

Anything that touches the essence of who you are, triggering your desire to be all that you are meant to be is inspiration to the spiritual body. It is a great feeling! Your spirit needs inspiration every day. If you take care of this, it will be easier to take care of the rest of the needs of your body. In fact, when people ignore their spiritual bodies, they begin to lose their desire to do anything. Especially anything that requires extra effort.

L. You mean we don't have to learn through pain? There is another way?

G. Pain is certainly one of your favorite ways to learn. But I recommend it only as a last choice. This is about heaven on earth, not hell on earth! You can learn about life from watching a tennis match, a round of golf, or even a basketball or baseball game.

Your spirit thrives in love. When you are filled with love, it is pretty amazing what you can do. Love comes in many forms. This is important for you to know. Learning about these different forms is going to be a big part of this book. Many of you ignore your spiritual bodies. You are starving them to death. No wonder many of you are depressed and wandering through life with no idea of where you are going or even of the magnificent being that you are. You have no sense of mission, of why you are here. But I am here now to help you understand your spiritual body and what it needs so that you can begin to nourish it and allow it to be the power it is meant to be in your life.

To be healthy and strong the spiritual body needs:
1. **Hope**
2. **Gratitude and appreciation**
3. **Compassion**
4. **Sense of mission (why am I here?), knowing you are contributing to the higher good**
5. **Inspiration**
6. **Forgiveness**
7. **Support of like souls**
8. **Quiet time/silence**
9. **Unconditional love**

L. Is that all? That doesn't seem so hard. In fact, it seems like a pretty good prescription. So if we fill our spirit with these nine things, we will be "full of spirit," so to speak?

G. That's right! By the way, I like your sense of humor!

L. Thank You, I think! I have a question about number seven, "Support of like souls." What does that mean?

G. The spiritual body needs support from like souls—peers. But not necessarily from an age perspective. By peers, I mean souls that resonate. That are coming from the same place. You will observe in your lives that there are certain people that you feel immediately comfortable with upon meeting them. You feel as if you understand each other at a deeper level. With these people, your conversations are different from any that you have with other people. You feel a sense of support when you have spent time with them. You can tell them anything, without fear of judgment. They seem to know you, the real you! It is nourishing for you to be with them.

L. Yes, I see what You mean. There are people I feel at home with when we are together. I know that it is important for me to stay connected with them. That leads me to another question. Why does the spiritual body need forgiveness? And whom are we forgiving?

G. I'm glad you asked that. Forgiveness is much needed in your spiritual body, yet it is much misunderstood.

Your spirit needs forgiveness to heal.

Forgiveness for yourself as well as forgiveness for others. Forgiveness itself nourishes the spirit. Healing is inherent in forgiveness. Without the energy of forgiveness,

you hang on to your experiences. You relive them over
and over again. Something that happened a long time ago
affects your system today. It drains your energy today as if
it were actually happening today. Forgiveness is a powerful tool for realizing your true spirit! It truly enables you
to experience each moment that you are in.

Forgiveness is one path to living in the present moment.

L. What are the main characteristics of the spiritual body?

G. The spiritual body:

1. **Is linked closely to the emotional body and often
   heard through the heart.**
2. **Is easily wounded.**
3. **Leaves the body if abused.**
4. **Is healed with love.**
5. **Must be healed so that the rest of the body can function at high levels (and if the wound is serious
   enough, to function at all).**
6. **Is powerful.**
7. **Is the closest link to soul.**
8. **Acts as a guiding light.**

L. Wow! I can see why care must be taken when dealing with
anyone's spirit. What are the main functions and purposes
of the spiritual body?

G. The main functions and purposes of the spiritual body:

1. **To inspire the body and anyone or anything that comes into its awareness.**
2. **To link you with Higher Power and higher meaning in your life.**
3. **The driving force in the body.**

L. I can see why the spiritual body is important. It is a part of our everyday lives as much as it is a part of the grand and dramatic moments in our lives. This is good stuff!

G. Thank you! What did you expect?

L. I wasn't expecting You! But I'm glad You came.

G. I was always here.

L. I'm getting tired. I thought maybe You would keep me going somehow and I wouldn't get tired.

G. That would be violating one of the needs of the body. Sleep! We'll start again tomorrow morning. Whenever you are ready, I'll be here.

L. God night! I meant to say "Good night." How do I know You're not just a figment of my imagination?

G. You don't! I thought you were going to sleep? Do what I tell you to do, and find out for yourself. Experiment! Isn't that how you've always done it anyway? You never have been one to believe someone else's experience without substantiating it on your own. If it doesn't work for you, what difference does it make to you where it came from? The origin is not what's important. When it works for you it becomes of value to you. That is what matters anyway. Besides, do you really believe all this information is coming from you?

L. I don't know. It feels like it is. Then again, I am sure it isn't. It is so clear when it is You speaking. There is no doubt, just knowing.

G. Your questions are flowing freer now.

L. I feel centered. And I am very happy. I have so much energy. This is the first time that I have felt the energy around my book. I feel it is coming into form. That is exciting to me. I have been talking and writing about this book for so long that I was beginning to wonder whether it would ever get done. I even wondered why I was bothering to work so hard on it. Now, it is fun. You are perfect for me!

G. Thank you! I feel the same about you!

L. Wow! I can feel myself engulfed in love. It is as if I am totally safe in this love. It doesn't matter what is happening on the outside of me. From where I am, everything is perfect as it is. All is right with the world. My energy is flowing freely. My body is singing. I wish my voice could sing like that.

G. Then you would be singing this book, instead of writing it. Yet your voice does sing. When you use your voice in your work, it is a form of song.

L. I do feel You with me. It isn't lonely writing as it usually is. But I don't really know You.

G. Then get to know me. I am here for you. I am here for everyone.

L. Seems impossible to be here for everyone. I want to be able to help everyone, but how can I? After all, You did say I was like You!

G. You are helping everyone. You help everyone by helping the person in front of you. One person at a time. One moment at a time. The ripples go out. Look at Princess Diana.

Look at Mother Teresa. They have shown you the way. Follow and lead at the same time.

L. I do know. I just get lost some times. It does feel good to be in touch with my spirit. The importance of nourishing it and giving it attention is obvious.

G. Yes! If you take care of your spirit, the rest will follow.

Review of the Spiritual Body
Needs

1. Hope
2. Gratitude and appreciation
3. Compassion
4. Sense of mission (why am I here?), knowing you are contributing to the higher good
5. Inspiration
6. Forgiveness
7. Support of like souls
8. Quiet time/silence
9. Unconditional love

Main Characteristics

1. Is linked closely to the emotional body and often heard through the heart.
2. Is easily wounded.
3. Leaves the body if abused.
4. Is healed with love.
5. Must be healed so the rest of the body can function at high levels (and if the wound is serious enough, to function at all).
6. Is powerful.
7. Is the closest link to soul.
8. Acts as a guiding light.

Main Functions and Purposes

1. To inspire
2. To link you with Higher Power and higher meaning in your life.
3. The driving force in the body.

Highlights

1. Forgiveness is an inner tool.

2. Your spirit needs forgiveness to heal.

3. Forgiveness means forgiving yourself as well as all others.

4. Forgiveness is one path that brings you to the present.

3

The Mental Body

G. This is where many people get into trouble. The mind plays tricks on you. It too is powerful. The mental body fuels the emotional body. Creation, whether of a project or an action, begins with a thought, an idea, a whim, an inkling, a glimpse of something possible.

L. That's why we need to be aware of our thoughts. We need to be able to choose wisely.

G. Or at least be aware of what you are choosing, so that you know what you are creating. Then you can ask yourself, before you go too far down a certain path, whether that really is what you want to be creating in your life.

L. Does the mental body have needs like the spiritual body does?

G. Yes, of course. Some are quite different from the needs of the spiritual body, but some are the same.

L. What are they?

G. **The mental body needs:**

1. **Discipline** (Or it will go all over the place. It can go to the past, present, or future in a flash. It can go to a different place, a different world.)
2. **Direction** (You need to be in charge of your thoughts.)
3. **Clear intent** (Mixed signals cause confusion.)
4. **Silence between thoughts**
5. **Quiet time/meditation**
6. **Complete expression and freedom of its ideas**
7. **Safety and acceptance in its expression**
8. **Mental activity** (It thrives on new ideas and thoughts. Are you bored? Your mental body probably needs nourishment.)

L. Those seem a little harder than what the spirit needs. It sounds like the mental body needs to be free to fully express itself, yet it needs discipline, too.

G. It does need discipline. If you learn to discipline your mind, it will come to be something you can use. If you don't, it will use you. It is like a child. A child needs guidance.

That's what discipline is—just a form of guidance.

Watch a two-year-old child. She wants to do everything, get into everything, and try everything. She gets into quite a bit of trouble if there isn't someone there to guide her. Discipline has gotten a bad rap. When used correctly, it is a tool that makes your life run smoother. It is meant to feel good. All your tools are meant to help you feel good, to keep your energy flowing freely. Unencumbered. Remember: you are in charge of your thoughts.

Your thoughts are powerful because you give them power.

Thoughts in and of themselves are just that—thoughts. It is when you give them energy that they become a creative force in your life. Because you have not been disciplining your thoughts, they have gotten quite out of hand. You have begun to believe your thoughts simply because you think them—rather than because they are thoughts you have consciously or unconsciously chosen. Thoughts have power when you give them power, not before. It is your thinking something that makes it true for you. Not because it is true in and of itself.

L. This is a topic we could spend a lot of time discussing. What did You mean by our thoughts encumbering us? Encumbering us by what?

G. By fear. We'll get into that later.

L. Couldn't we talk about fear now?

G. We could. It has been one of your topics lately, hasn't it?

L. Yes! Is fear what blocks us from reaching our goals?

G. You have been learning about fear, just as you have been learning about love. We'll get to it soon enough. Rest assured. Let's stay on track. You did say you wanted to complete this book, didn't you?

L. Yes, I do! Okay, back to the mental body. The mental body needs discipline, direction, clear intent, and silence. The spiritual body needs silence, too!

G. Remember, the bodies are interdependent, and so all of the bodies will need some of the same things. When you are silent, you nourish the whole system. You feel its effects all over you. Bliss is one of the results. Go on, what else does the mental body need?

L. It needs complete expression and freedom of ideas. It needs to be safe and accepted in its expression. And it needs new thoughts and ideas. It sounds like it thrives on itself.

G. Yes, it does. Ideas create more ideas and so on and on and on. Can you see why discipline is so important? Since the mental body needs complete expression and freedom of this expression of its ideas, you want to be sure that you are expressing what you really want to express. You want to choose the thoughts you have. They lead to thought patterns. Thought patterns lead to ideas. Once you have an idea, your mental body will want to express it. Completely!

L. In other words, be careful what I think?

G. Yes! You become the thoughts you hold onto. The thoughts you think most often. The quality of your thoughts determines the quality of your life. Simple enough?

L. Yes. But why is that so hard to understand? I mean if we really got it, wouldn't we be thinking only positive, life-enhancing thoughts?

G. Yes. But often, there is a space between when you think a thought and when it manifests into form.

Because of this space between thought and manifestation, you lose sight of the direct link between your thoughts and the form they take in your life.

If you could manifest into form all your thoughts right now, do you realize what your life would be like? How often do you change your mind? How often do you think something in the heat of the moment that you don't mean later? How often do you wish for something one moment and not want it the next? Listen to your prayers. Do you really want all that stuff you ask for? You don't know what you want most of the time. That is what I have been telling you through the ages. Know thyself. How often have you heard yourself say, "I don't know what I want?" This causes you more problems than anything else does. If you don't know yourself, how can you know what you want, what is right for you?

L.   So if we learn how the body functions, we learn more about ourselves.

G.   Yes. Even though you are not your body, it is through experiencing the physical world with the challenge of doing it in a body that you will go to deeper levels of love. And the more you will know yourself.

L.   That makes sense. What are the main characteristics of the mental body?

G.   **The main characteristics of the mental body are:**

1.   **It can hold only one thought at a time.**
2.   **It can go all over the place.** (Past, present, future. Different locations. Your physical body can be playing tennis on one court while your mental body is off watching someone else on another court. Or in another place altogether different from where the physical body is.)

3. Once it is presented with a question or a problem, it works toward solution until it gets a new command, thought or question. (In sport, you will see an athlete ask a question, often in exasperation. Then off goes the mental body to figure out the answer, taking the athlete out of the present moment.)

Of course, to perform at high levels, you must be in the present. Knowing that when asked a question the mental body will go off and figure out the answer, tells you that during competition you must be aware of the questions you are asking of yourself.

L. I have seen that cause lots of problems for athletes during competition. Is it the same off the playing field?

G. Yes, of course. Remember what I said about sport being one way of learning about life in a body? What applies in competition applies in life!

L. So we want to be aware of the questions we are asking ourselves. I know that the right question can take me a long way towards solving a problem. My friend Bryce Young always asks, "What is my next, best possible, move?"

G. Your friend asks a good question. Can you see how that question keeps you moving forward?

L. Yes! It is much better than asking some other questions that people find themselves asking—questions that only seem to keep us stuck. Like "Why did I do that?" From what You said about how the mental body works, the mind would have a field day with that question.

G. Oh yes! It would give you every possible answer you can imagine. Most of which wouldn't make you feel very good!

I wouldn't ask that question unless you can answer it right away. When you do something you wish you hadn't, you don't need negative thoughts blocking your energy even more.

L. So this is where discipline comes in! I can see how important it is to guide our thoughts. They do go all over the place! I think we need to know what function the mental body serves so that we can use it more efficiently.

What are the main functions and purposes of the mental body?

G. **The main functions and purposes of the mental body are:**

1. **To think**
2. **To solve problems**
3. **To find answers to questions**
4. **To fuel the emotional body**
5. **To begin the creative process in the physical world**

L. That's seems obvious enough.

G. It is. Yet you see people using their mental bodies for functions that need perhaps the emotional body or the spiritual body. The more you understand the purpose and function of each body, the easier it is to use the appropriate body for the situation. For instance, when your partner says "I love you," it is time to use your emotional body. Just let yourself feel the expression of love. But how often do you start thinking, instead of just feeling?

Review of the Mental Body
Needs

1. Discipline
2. Direction
3. Clear Intent
4. Silence
5. Quiet time/Meditation
6. Complete expression and freedom of its ideas
7. Safety and acceptance in its expression
8. Mental activity

Main Characteristics

1. It can hold only one thought at a time.
2. It can go all over the place.
3. Once it is presented with a question or a problem, it goes to work to solve it.

Main Functions and Purposes

1. To think
2. To solve problems
3. To find answers to questions
4. To fuel the emotional body
5. To begin the creative process in the physical world

Highlights

1. Discipline is a form of guidance.

2. Your thoughts are powerful because you give them power.

3. Thoughts require energy to become a creative force.

4. The four bodies (spiritual, mental, emotional, and physical) are interdependent.

5. Thought quality determines life quality.

6. Ask "what is my next best possible move?" to keep moving forward.

4

The Emotional Body

L. Women use their emotional bodies more than men do. Is that true?

G. No, that is a misconception. You all use your emotional bodies, whether you are aware of it or not. Men in your world have been taught to use their mental bodies more than their emotional bodies. But women, as well, have a hard time using their emotional bodies correctly. For they, too, have been taught how to use their mental bodies but not how to use their emotional bodies.

L. We seem to know so little about it. What does the emotional body need?

G. I think you'll find out that the emotional body is pretty interesting!

Okay, the emotional body needs:

1. **Full expression of its feelings and emotions**
2. **Acceptance and nonjudgment**
3. **Safety in expressing its feelings and emotions**

   4. **Understanding**
   5. **Trust**
   6. **Love**
   7. **To feel**

L. I see that the needs of the emotional body are similar to the needs of the mental body. Full expression, acceptance, and safety are needs of the mental body, too. What are the main characteristics of the emotional body?

G. **The main characteristics of the emotional body are that:**

   1. **Repressed or unresolved emotions and experiences can be triggered at any time.**
   2. **Emotions and feelings are always felt in the present, as if they are happening now**
   3. **Emotions and feelings can engulf you, as if they are permanent and all-consuming.**
   4. **Feelings and emotions pass through and out of the body when allowed full expression.**
   5. **Emotions are fueled by the mental body.**
   6. **Emotions often express themselves through the heart (chakra).** (When expressing something from the heart or emotional body, to others or yourself, you feel the expression or energy in your heart area.)
   7. **This expression can enhance or deplete your energy.**
   8. **Unexpressed feelings and emotions get trapped in the physical body, causing distress or disease in the body.**

L. What You are saying is that we need to express our feelings just as we need to express our thoughts. And that we need to be aware of our feelings, emotions, and experiences because, when repressed, they can cause havoc in our bodies.

G. Feelings and emotions are very powerful. Your body is a work of art, if I do say so myself! From your spirit to your thoughts to your feelings and emotions, they are all pieces of the puzzle that make up your body.

L. I can see that when You talk about it this way. It all begins to make more sense. So what are the main functions and purposes of the emotional body?

G. **The main functions and purposes of the emotional body are:**

1. **To feel** (Imagine loving someone or something without feeling love, only thinking it.)
2. **To energize the physical body, through the correct use of emotions, to higher levels of performance**
3. **To motivate**
4. **To move the physical body to action**

L. Well, that brings up another one of my questions. Where does motivation come from?

G. Motivation comes from the heart. That's why athletes need to learn about the heart and spirit to play or perform at top levels. In fact, when athletes play with their hearts instead of their heads, they have a much easier time directing their bodies to do what they have been training them to do. The channel will be clear from the head to the heart to the body.

Power comes from the heart!

L. I see that all the time. If the heart isn't in something, it just doesn't work out very well. Okay, so we have our hearts in it, but the spirit keeps it going. Isn't that right?

G. Yes! Inspiration comes from the spiritual body.

L. We saw quite the example of that in the 1996 U.S. Tennis Open. Pete Sampras was playing Alex Corretja. Pete was in the fifth-set tiebreaker. Sick. Actually throwing up on the court. He said after the match that he just wanted it to be over so that he could get out of there. His heart wanted out, yet he stayed. What kept him there playing?

G. His spirit, of course. He was on his path.

Review of the Emotional Body

Needs

1. Full expression of its feelings and emotions
2. Acceptance and nonjudgment
3. Safety in expressing feelings and emotions
4. Understanding
5. Trust
6. Love
7. To feel

Main Characteristics

1. Repressed or unresolved emotions and experiences can be triggered at any time.
2. Emotions and feelings are always felt in the present.
3. Emotions can feel totally consuming
4. Feelings and emotions pass through the body when allowed full expression.
5. Emotions are fueled by the mental body.
6. Expression is felt in the heart area.
7. This expression either enhances or depletes your energy.
8. Unexpressed feelings and emotions get trapped in the body, causing dis-ease or distress in the body.

Main Functions and Purposes

1. To feel
2. To energize the physical body
3. To motivate
4. To move the physical body to action

Highlights

1. Motivation comes from the heart.

2. Power comes from the heart.

5

The Physical Body

L. I don't know what is wrong with me. I feel like I'm drag-
    ging. My energy is low, and I just can't get myself going.
G. Take a couple of deep breaths. Let yourself settle into your
    body. When you haven't been filling all your fuel tanks,
    your energy gets depleted. We've covered the spiritual,
    mental, and emotional bodies. It's time to discuss the physi-
    cal body.

The basic needs of the physical body are:

1. **Fuel** (Food and light are fuel for your body.)
2. **Water** (at least eight glasses a day)
3. **Sleep** (Six to eight hours is a good guideline.)
4. **Oxygen** (Deep breathing is essential to life in a physi-
    cal body.)
5. **Movement** (Use it, or lose it!)
6. **Touch** (Massage is great, of course, but your own mas-
    saging of your body is even more important.)
7. **Love** (How many of you hate the appearance of your
    bodies?)

L. That's it? Just those seven things? That doesn't seem too complicated!

G. It isn't. But don't let its simplicity fool you. Your body is a wonderful vehicle for you.

L. Why does the body need touch?

G. When you touch your skin with loving touch, you turn on the healing and recovery system in your body. You are meant to heal and recover easily and naturally. You just need to activate the healing energy. Touch is one of your most powerful tools. So much so that your body needs it. Not wants it, needs it. Many of you are suffering from touch deprivation because you think the touch has to come from someone else. I am telling you that this is not true. You need to be the one who is activating the healing. Others can help you. But if you are not sending love to all the cells in your body on a regular basis, they will have a hard time staying healthy and strong.

L. Are there any other benefits from touch?

G. Besides that it feels good?

L. Yes.

G. Yes, there are. When you are treating your body with love through touch, it becomes harder and harder to mistreat your body. It will be easier to choose the right fuel in the right amount. You will take better care of a body you love. Oh, yes, Linda. Love has many benefits, and it begins with loving your body.

L. That makes sense. If I don't love my body, I certainly won't take good care of it. In fact, it probably would be pretty easy to abuse it. What are the main characteristics of the physical body?

G. The main characteristics of the physical body are that it:

1. Gets its direction from the mental, emotional and spiritual components
2. Is conscious and aware
3. Comes in different shapes, sizes, colors, and appearances
4. Changes shape
5. Can heal and recover
6. Experiences the physical world

L. I guess those are pretty obvious. What are the main functions and purposes of the physical body? Or are those obvious, too?

G. Yes, of course they are obvious too. Perhaps, they are worth mentioning anyway. Sometimes, it is the obvious that eludes you.

The main functions and purposes of the physical body are:

1. To take you where ever you want to go (movement)
2. To give you the experiences of life in a physical body (such as touch, smell, sight, hearing, and taste)
3. To give you information about your world (You experience your feelings in your body. You receive feedback.)
4. To experience sacred union with another person
5. To create other human beings
6. To learn about love in a physical body
7. To express love

L. Hmmm! That is worth hearing. I guess it's not quite so obvious as I thought. How do we express love in our physical bodies?

G. Your body language is always expressing or denying love. How you move towards or away from someone can be an expression of love or of fear. Where your body takes you. Where you choose to be. What you choose to do with your body. What you do with your eyes and ears. How you treat your body or other bodies. These are all expressions of love or fear.

L. So a movement towards someone can be an expression of love?

G. Yes. Using your body to send an e-mail message to your son is an expression of love.

L. I thought that came from my heart.

G. It did. But first you had the thought. You fed the thought to your emotional body, which opened up to desire. Desire to express in some way your love. Desire moved your physical body to do the typing of the letter and sending of the message. Without the physical body, that form of manifestation of love could not have been possible. Do you not enjoy all the ways you can use your body to express love?

L. Yes, I do. I guess I just didn't quite think of it in those terms. But I see now how we use our bodies to express love. Awhile ago, on a road trip with the tennis team, Tracy made cookies for the team, as well as bringing different fruits. She used her hands to express love in the preparation of the food.

G. Yes, she did it beautifully, didn't she?

L. I was amazed! She was able to express love in so many ways. It was very nice to be around her.

G. Love is always nice to be around!

L. How else do we use our bodies to express love?

G. Your athletes are a good example. They use their bodies to play the sport they love. When they stay in love, their bodies perform at incredible levels. Love is the fuel to higher and higher performance. You will hear more and more about athletes playing with heart and spirit! It is the path to greatness in everything you do.

L. Of course! That fits with why I am always saying, "Play with your heart." They have a hard time doing that. They seem to think it is important to play with their heads.

G. Unfortunately they will not find the essence of their sport in their heads. Games are meant to be fun. They are meant to be played because you love the game. From this love of the game you are able to inspire your body to soar in whatever sport you have chosen. It is what you do when you go for a walk. You tune into how good your body feels when it gets the movement it needs to be healthy and strong.

L. If movement is so important for our bodies, why do so many people have a hard time exercising regularly?

G. Because they go to their mental bodies when it is time to workout. They have perhaps worked hard all day at a desk job. Their minds are tired. So they ask themselves, "Should I go work out?" Remember, it is the job of your mental body to answer questions. It can answer questions in any way possible! Since often it is your mental body that is tired, it responds, "No, I'm too tired." Well, now you know that your physical body isn't too tired. It didn't do anything all day. So, as regards to working out, you just do. No questions asked. The answer is always yes, so you don't need to ask the question.

L. I get it! It's like brushing teeth. We just do it. I don't get up in the morning and ask, "Should I brush my teeth today?" I just do it!

G. That's right. Asking the question implies that no is a possible answer. It gives you a 50-50 chance of coming up with no. If you want to stay on a workout program, never ask the question, or if you do, always answer "yes" before you can think of all the reasons that you don't want to work out today.

L. I can see how important it is to know the functions of all the bodies. We seem to misuse them quite a bit.

G. Yes, but now you can use them as they were meant to be used.

L. Is it really that easy?

G. Yes, it is.

L. Why do we make it so hard then?

G. You do, don't you? It is because you didn't know all the needs and functions of your whole body. Now you do. You have no excuse!

L. I don't want excuses. We have argued enough for our misery!

G. It is up to you. You can live in your body as you see fit. It is always your choice. I want you to know how your body is meant to help you experience and discover love. Discover you!

L. Are we creating our physical bodies even as grown-ups?

G. Yes, of course! You know that you are. Your thoughts and emotions help form your body.

L. How does the spiritual body come into all of this?

G. Again, your spiritual body is the driving force. Without your spirit, you would not live in a physical body for very long. Your spirit is your connection to your soul. You hear the messages of your soul through your spirit. And you hear the message of your spirit through your heart. You are on a journey. Enjoy it! That is why you chose it!

L. I think we need to talk a little more about the inner tools You are always referring to.

G. Have you no more questions about the physical body? After all, this is a book about living in a body!

L. Yes, I know! But I am more interested in the mental, emotional, and spiritual bodies and how they affect and interact with the physical body. These are the kinds of questions I get in my work. We already have a lot of information about the physical body.

G. All right, you're the boss!

L. No, wait a minute. You're the boss.

G. No, Linda. You have free will. You are the boss. You can create your life however you desire.

L. Sometimes You are so ungodlike!

G. How can I be ungodlike? I can never be something that I am not. I am. All that I am, I am.

L. I just felt this surge of energy, of love. It felt so good. Thank You.

G. You are welcome.

L. Why can't I feel Your love like that all the time?

G. You can.

L. How?

G. By coming from love yourself. By tuning into it. By expecting it. By knowing it is with you all the time. By trusting. By living your life in joy. Take this love and use your many opportunities to express this love to others.

Review of the Physical Body
Needs

1. Fuel
2. Water
3. Sleep
4. Oxygen
5. Movement
6. Touch
7. Love

Main Characteristics

1. Receives direction from the mental, emotional and spiritual components
2. Is conscious and aware
3. Comes in different shapes, sizes, colors, and appearances
4. Changes shape
5. Can heal and recover
6. Experiences the physical world

Main Functions and Purposes

1. To take you wherever you want to go
2. To experience life in a body
3. Feedback
4. To experience sacred union with another person
5. To create other human beings
6. To learn about love in a physical body
7. To express love

Highlights

1. Health and healing come from sending love to all your body's cells.

2. Your body language is always expressing or denying love.

3. Love is the physical body's fuel to higher performance.

6

When Doubt Is Love

G. Did you feel my presence with you last week at the symposium on Hilton Head?

L. Oh, yes! It's true. I felt Your presence with me. I knew this time. Or I guess it would be more accurate to say that I acted in this knowing. I always know. What a difference it made. The love was so strong.

G. And your speech? How did it go this time?

L. Which one?

G. Which one would you like to speak of?

L. Both of them. I was amazed. Yes, You are right. I want to speak of both of them, but I am most pleased about the speech about fear.

G. Tell me about it.

L. Okay. The title of my talk was "Fear: Playing the Ultimate Opponent." When I spoke on this topic in the past, I found it difficult because I felt so much fear while I was preparing and before I got up to speak. I then had to change my state in order to speak at all.

This time I prepared for my talk not by writing down notes or planning what I was going to say. I knew, of course, the topic and the essence of what I wanted to share with people. So I took time to be silent. I lay on my bed. Alone. I asked You for guidance, stating what I wanted to do in my talk. I expressed my desire to help people. I anchored that awareness. I was doing my speech because I believed it was part of my mission to do so. Then I bathed myself in light and love. I didn't think. I just bathed in the Light and Love.

G. And how did this work?

L. The room was overflowing. People were sitting on the floor because there weren't enough seats. I stayed in my heart. They were mesmerized. As was I. I spoke almost the whole time from a higher energy level. The energy in the room was beautiful.

G. And what did you learn?

L. I am still learning. I know now that when I am asked to speak, it is not only the words I speak that are important. It is the energy behind the words. Of course it makes sense to me now. My mission is to help people to know love. What better way to help them experience love than while I am speaking of fear?

G. Now you have it! Good work! I am enjoying your process. You are quite the creation, if I do say so myself!

L. Thank You!

G. You're welcome. To know love while in fear . . .

L. Well, I thought I could only know one or the other. I thought fear blocked love. I have obviously gotten it wrong. Help me to understand.

G. Different situations ask for different forms of love. Remember, however, the essence of all your inner tools is love. So, no matter which one you choose, you are essentially choosing love. Fear is merely love in disguise. You said that fear is tricky. That it disguises itself, sometimes even disguises itself as love. You were on the right track. Fear is love disguised. Disguised as doubt. Disguised as anger. Disguised as frustration. Disguised as impatience.

L. I don't understand what You are saying. I am confused. Fear is love disguised? Please help me to understand what that means. I thought fear was the opposite of love.

G. You are right when you say that fear is energy that is blocked or scattered. And love is energy that is flowing freely. This helps you to feel the effects of your thoughts in your energy system. Now, listen closely. Energy is neither good nor bad. Neither fear nor love. Those are words that describe the effects of your thoughts and intentions.

Fear, in moments of opportunity, as you said in your speech, is love, too. For example, the doubt that you may feel before doing something is there for a reason. Doubt is fear, from an energy perspective, in that it does block your energy. It is blocking your energy for a reason. All of what you call "negative" feelings are there to protect you.

I am Love. All that is comes from this Source. All is Love.

The reason you call these "negative" feelings bad is that you use your tools at the wrong times. You use them for the wrong reasons.

L. What do You mean by wrong?

51

G.   Your intention is to do something. To accomplish what you set as your intention, you will need certain "inner tools." These tools help you achieve your goal.

When you choose a tool that does not help you achieve the result you desire, you have chosen the "wrong" tool.

That is all. It is not a judgment of the value of the tool. If you used a golf club to play tennis, you would be using the "wrong" equipment or the wrong tool to play tennis. It is the same with "inner tools." They all have a purpose. When you use the wrong inner tool, you judge the tool to be bad because you didn't get the result you wanted. But there is nothing wrong with the tool. Choosing the correct tool is what is important.

Doubt is as much a tool as confidence is.

L.   How can doubt be a tool? What good is it? Doesn't it have to have a "use" in order to be a tool?

G.   Yes, of course! That is the inherent nature in tools. They are meant to help you.

L.   But how can doubt be of any help? It just seems to hold people back. I know many people who don't achieve what they desire because they doubt themselves.

G.   Listen to what you just said. Repeat it. The last part.

L.   They doubt themselves?

G.   Yes! That is exactly how people misuse the tool of doubt. Doubt is not meant to be used to doubt oneself. You are. I am. There is no doubt about that. We are! That you can and are sure of.

L.   Am I?

G. Yes, you are. Right now, stop what you are doing, thinking, feeling, and say aloud or silently, I AM. Again. I AM. I AM. I AM. I AM. I AM. Do you feel it? I AM. YOU ARE. Have no doubt. You are.

L. Now, I get it. We are using doubt to doubt ourselves. Of course it doesn't feel right, because we know we are! So what is the use of doubt? If doubt is love disguised, what is the essence of doubt?

G. **Doubt is meant to be used when you are:**

1. **On the wrong track—headed in the wrong direction.** It is a compass of sorts. To track your physical whereabouts you use a compass. To track the direction you are going when headed for a goal, doubt is the tool that lets you know you have taken a wrong turn.

2. **To strengthen you when you begin a new direction or take a different path.** It is meant to aid you in asking yourself the right questions. The questions that you need to answer in order to know whether what you are doing or where you are going is really what you want to do or where you want to go.

L. I get it! My friend Pam does this with me all the time. I'll tell her about something I want to do. But I'm not sure whether I know how to do it, whether it is the right thing to do, whether I have the courage to do it, or even whether I really want to do it. She will start asking me questions. She plays the "devil's advocate." It helps me to clarify my feelings and my position.

G. Your friend is a wise woman! She is helping you to use the tool of doubt correctly. Doubt is meant to give you the opportunity to pause and assess your situation. Are you on the right track? Are you going in the right direction? Do you really want to do it? Do you really want to have it? All these questions arise with the tool of doubt.

L. Now I see how doubt strengthens me. When You first said that, I thought I misunderstood You. I have always thought of doubt as something that weakens me.

G. All of your inner tools are meant to strengthen you. Everything has a reason for its existence. All is of worth. Just as everyone is of worth.

Highlights

1. All is love.

2. Fear is love disguised.

3. Energy is neither "good" nor "bad."

4. Everything has a purpose.

5. Doubt is a tool that lets you know you are on the wrong track or that strengthens you in your new direction.

7

Food Is Not Your Only Fuel

L. What if everything I believe to be true isn't? What if my perception is just that, my perception. Maybe I am just making everything up.

G. Whoa! Slow down. First of all, you are right that it is just your perception. It is your perception of what happened that is important in your world. It is always that way. How one perceives a situation or experience is unique to each individual. Your perceptions are helpful and important to share with others so that they may also open up to another way of perceiving the experience. There are many ways you could experience your life, depending on where you put your focus.

L. I don't know where this is going. What are we doing today? I feel out of sync.

G. That's because you are, again, filled with answers. Empty yourself of the answers, and fill yourself instead with the questions you have. I will give you the answers. That is why you called on me, isn't it?

L. Yes! I like talking to You like this. It is the closest I have ever felt to You.

G. Why do you do that?

L. Do what?

G. Capitalize any reference to me?

L. To symbolize that You are God.

G. Capitalizing doesn't make me who I am. It means nothing to me. It only slows you down. People know to whom you are referring. I won't be offended.

L. Who are you?

G. This book isn't about who I am. This is about who you are. It is about you in a body. It is about love in a body. Let's save who I am for another book.

L. There are more books?

G. Yes, did you want to put it all in one book? That would be a pretty big book. You know who I am. Never forget that. You know. And so do all the people reading these words. When you get into defining me, putting labels on me, trying to figure out who I am, you get lost. You lose sight of who I am. Stay in knowing. You need not figure me out to know me. All you need to do to know me is turn inward and feel me with you, always. Feel the safety, the strength, and the love when you tune into me.

Do not place labels on me. Each of you knows me in your own way and experiences me in your own way. When you open up to me, you know me. That is all that matters, isn't it?

L. Yes! I just get curious.

G. No, it is not curiosity that asks the question. It is doubt. You doubt me. You doubt yourself. Am I? Are you? Go inside, Linda, and ask these questions. That is where the answers are. Have you not felt my presence all weekend? Do you not feel my presence now? Have you not known me though you can't find quite the right words to describe me? I am love. Of that you can be sure!

Well, we diverge. But then that is how life is. You start out on one path only to discover another and another and another. Follow the energy of the moment. It is the way of life. Tell me, now, what is your perception of the weekend you just spent with the tennis team?

L. Okay! I knew I was in the right place. I knew that being with the team was where I was supposed to be. It was easier to see what they were experiencing. It was even clearer than last year. Why is that?

G. Because you are clearer. You have asked to see. Your intent was clear. You knew why you were there. You know who you are. When you come from who you are, your experiences take on a whole new life. You find yourself living every moment. The moment you are in is the moment that is important. You are not in the past or in the future. You are totally there. All of you. You are powerful.

Also, you came from your heart. When you come from your heart, you hear the voice of your soul, and without much fanfare, you move from your heart to your soul. You experience life from your soul's perspective. You cannot go wrong when you live your life from your soul's desire. What you call your mission is the voice of your soul. That is why it is so important to hear your soul's voice. But let's get back to the body.

You work with athletes. Athletes who want their bodies to perform at a high level.

L. Yes, how does the body raise its level of performance? What is the trick?

G. It is no trick. It is a matter of giving the body clear instructions. It responds to every thought, every command, and every direction you give it. That is how it was created. You have everything you need within you.

You need to know what instructions turn on the engine, how to keep it running smoothly, how to accelerate it, how to smooth it out, and how to heal and recover.

L. Good. This is what everyone wants to know. How does this body function?

G. The first thing you need to know is that these instructions are meant to be followed all the time. By all of you. Not just for athletes competing in an athletic event. Yet you can learn a lot from athletes. They are in a position to demonstrate to others what the body is capable of doing.

L. But it seems like they don't know all that much about how to take care of their bodies. So many of them abuse their bodies. They put their bodies through pure torture. They don't seem to have a true understanding of how to treat their bodies. They are often frustrated and impatient with themselves. It is not a pretty sight. Yet some of them do perform with this kind of treatment. Why is that?

G. Certain people have chosen bodies that allow them to be in this position to teach by demonstration.

L. Oh, I am having a hard time with this. I can't believe athletes are our role models.

G. What you just described is not the role model I have been discussing. Athletes are reflecting life. They are reflecting the path that society has been choosing. The path of fear. This is not how it is meant to be.

Athletes are meant to show you how to live in love. How to use tools that reflect love, not fear. In order for their bodies to perform at higher levels, athletes need to learn how to come from love when they are performing. Just as all of you are to come from love. In all that you do. That is the purpose of sport. One of the easiest ways to learn how to use your inner tools is through sport.

L. What do you mean? How does sport teach us to use our inner tools? I know all about the teamwork stuff. But I have a feeling that you mean something else. I think we're finally getting back to the body and the "owner's manual." Let's go over how it works again. A quick review.

G. The mental body fuels the emotional body, the emotional body fuels the physical body, and the spiritual body is the force that keeps it going.

L. What do you mean by fuel? That seems to cause some confusion.

G. That is a good question. The kind of fuel that you use determines the level of performance of the body. Often athletes use the right fuel. But just as often they use fuel that does not help the body to raise its level of performance but instead lowers it.

L. What kind of fuel are you talking about? I know you don't mean food. Do you? There are already enough books about nutrition.

G. Well, your body certainly needs food. But no, that isn't the kind of fuel I'm referring to. As we talked about earlier, each of the bodies needs their own special fuel. One of the problems you have with your body is that you use the same fuel for every situation and hunger you have.

L. Please continue.

G. There are times when your body does need food. It lets you know with hunger pangs. You recognize that signal quite easily. The problem is that if it isn't food that your body needs, you don't know what to give it. Earlier we talked about the needs of the mental, emotional, and spiritual bodies.

These needs are the fuel to which I am referring. Once you understand and know how to determine what kind of fuel you need, you will learn how to live in peace.

You will be able to maintain the weight that is right for your body, be happy, and know love. You will be able to achieve the goals you desire. Your life will be transformed.

At first, it may appear on the outside that nothing has changed. However, on the inside, everything will have changed. And in time, you will notice the changes on the outside. Your relationships will be stronger and of greater depth. Your response to what would have been a stressful situation in the past will be totally different. You will respond with a calm, a sense of peace, and a sense of knowing that will please you more than you can imagine at this moment.

L. That is hard to believe! There are many difficult situations in our lives. Sometimes it seems like everything is going against us. We can't lose the weight we want to. We're not happy at our jobs. Kids are faced with incredible decisions. There are drugs, alcohol, sex, cigarettes, junk food, and violence.

G. Whoa, you're going down the path of doom! The path of no hope. Is that really where you want to go? The decisions that my children are faced with are always the same.

L. What do you mean, the same? They are up against so many more stressful situations than when I was a child.

G. Really? There were no drugs, no alcohol, no sex, no cigarettes, no junk food, and no violence when you were a child? Have you forgotten so much?

L. Okay! I get the idea!

G. Yes, Linda, it is about choices. It always has been. And the choice is always the same. Today, as it was yesterday.

L. How can that be? Kids have many more choices today than I did. More opportunities than I had.

G. The choice is still the same:

Is this something that strengthens your energy or something that depletes your energy?

That is always the choice. When you understand that, you will have come a long way to fulfilling the great potential inherent in your body. There are no limits to what your body can do. If you truly desire to do something you have the capacity to do it.

L. I'm sorry, but I have trouble with that. There are a lot of things I'd like to do, but can't. How can you say that?

G. When you really want to do something, you must be willing to commit to the actions required to get it done. If you want your book to be read and shared with people, you have to sit down and write it. You can't just talk about how much you want to get this book done. You have to do what it takes to accomplish it. If you want to excel in a certain sport, you have to train, to practice, to work out, to learn the rules, learn how to perform the sport, eat the kind of food that nourishes the body, and so on. Most people are not willing to do that. At least not for something that is not their heart's desire.

L. I know people who can't achieve their goals. Or who don't think they can achieve them and give up.

G. Exactly! You need to know how to achieve your goals. You must know your heart's desire. If it isn't your heart's desire, it will be tough to achieve it. Many of you work towards goals with little or no desire behind them.

L. Boy, is that true. I talk to a lot of people who have no idea what they want. And then, there are the people who know what they want, but can't get themselves to do it. What is that all about? Why is it so hard?

G. Is it so hard?

L. Yes! Just ask all those people out there who have dreams that never come true.

G. Or do you make it hard because you don't know another way? Another way that flows, that is filled with joy. The way of love.

You have been following the path of fear. Fear is always a difficult and painful path. It is impossible to achieve your goals living your life in fear.

L. Why is that?

G. Fear blocks your energy. That is its inherent quality. It is meant to block your energy. Living through love gets you on the right path, and keeps you on that path, making your dreams attainable.

Highlights

1. You hear the voice of your soul ultimately through your heart.

2. You can not go wrong when you listen to the voice of your soul.

3. The mental, emotional, and spiritual bodies need fuel, just as the physical body does.

4. Your choices either strengthen your energy or deplete your energy.

5. Fear used incorrectly either blocks or scatters your energy.

8

Fear As a Gift from God

G. Fear is a gift from God.

L. Wow! I didn't expect you to say that. You do surprise me
    at times.

G. I have to keep you on your toes. Keeps the interest up when
    you don't always know what is coming. You have done a
    lot of work to understand fear as well as you do. You dis-
    covered the gift of fear a long time ago.

L. Hmmm!

G. There are two ways to look at fear. One is from the per-
    spective of the body as a physical entity. The other is from
    the perspective of the body as energy and information. From
    the perspective of the physical, fear is an emotion. An
    emotion is a thought linked with a feeling or sensation in
    the body. That is the traditional definition. The second defi-
    nition goes a little deeper. It explains the effect of fear on
    the physical body as well as on your energy. Fear is energy
    that is blocked or scattered.

When you can see fear as blocked or scattered energy, you will have come a long way in discovering how to use the gift of fear.

L. All right. What is the purpose of fear? You said that it is a gift. You also said that everything has a purpose, a reason for its existence. How could fear possibly be good? It keeps people from achieving their goals. It even keeps them from fulfilling their mission.

G. Yes, that's true. But like so many of my tools, you misuse the tool of fear. Fear is meant to trigger your body's inner security system. When you are in danger from an outside source, your inner security system is triggered, and the command to "face the danger or flee" goes out. Let me repeat that, to "face the danger or flee."

   Notice I didn't say "fight" the danger. That is a different command. Fear does not signal the command to fight. In fact, fighting would be the wrong choice in most situations. You would be hard pressed to come up with very many examples of situations in your life today where fighting actually is the solution. The best solution anyway.

L. You're right, I can't.

G. Let me give you some examples of danger from an outside source. You're crossing the street, and don't see a car making a turn into your path. All of a sudden you are aware of the car roaring down on you. Fear triggers your inner security system, and your body moves quickly to get out of the way. Another example: you're walking down a dark street all by yourself when chills run up and down your back. You begin to run just to get out of there. You didn't see anyone or anything, but you felt the presence of danger from an outside source, and you responded to the danger by running. Another example: you come home, and as you put your key into the keyhole, you sense something is wrong. You leave and call the police. The police come, and you discover there was a burglar in your home. You felt your inner security system go off. It sent you the command to flee. Do you want more examples of fear from danger from an outside source?

L. No, I think that's enough. You know, I don't think we are in those situations very often, are we?

G. No, you aren't. The world is meant to be a safe place. Your body is a system of energy and information. When your energy is flowing freely, you feel strong, healthy, happy, and over all, pretty darn good. That is how you are meant to be. Your energy is meant to flow freely. You are supposed to feel good. By "wrong," I mean anything that doesn't move you toward your "goal" or fulfillment of your mission.

L. Okay, but you said fear blocks our energy. Isn't that wrong?

G. Not if it is giving you information that you need to decide your next move. Sometimes you do need to stop and assess your situation. You may have made a wrong turn. You need to correct it. You need to be aware that you are going in the wrong direction. It serves a useful purpose in these cases. Wouldn't you agree?

L. Yes, I can see that. Of course, it is like a safeguard.

G. That's it. I like that. A safeguard. Fear is meant to be a *safe guard*. Good work! When you use fear correctly it is not blocking your "energy." It is blocking you from doing something. Your energy is still flowing freely. When you use fear incorrectly, however, it blocks your "energy," which is totally different. That is when you have problems. When I say that fear blocks or scatters your energy, I am referring to the incorrect use of fear.

L. Oh, now I get it! I see the value of fear, the correct use of fear, that is. This certainly puts a different light on it. I never know for sure where we are going with our conversations. But I am enjoying our time together all the same.

G. As am I. Now, back to fear. We just briefly described fear in response to an outside danger. People have a pretty good understanding of this definition of fear. So let's move on to another kind—fear in moments of opportunity. This is where fear is used incorrectly.

Beware of fear in moments of opportunity that causes your energy to be blocked or scattered.

Whenever you are presented with an opportunity, your energy shifts. This shift in your energy is meant to prepare you for the opportunity. Opportunity calls for more of your energy. This alone can cause alarm, by the way. Many of you think you don't have enough energy to do what you want to do. So when this call goes out for more energy, you back away in fear. You block your energy. Or you scatter your energy all over the place in an attempt to keep from losing it. In these cases, moments of opportunity, your inner security system is triggered, just as when you were in danger from an outside source. This time, however, the danger is fear itself. The blocked or scattered energy is causing your problem. There is no real danger. "The only thing you have to fear is fear itself."

L. What a difference that makes. To see fear simply as energy that is blocked or scattered takes the wind out of fear's sails, I'd say.

G. That's right. Somewhere along the line these shifts in energy got misinterpreted. Before long, everyone was responding in similar ways.

Let's go over it again. This is how it works: When you are faced with an opportunity, your energy begins to build. This buildup feels a bit uncomfortable. It doesn't hurt. At least it isn't meant to hurt you. It just feels different. The information you apply to it determines whether or not your energy will continue building until the moment of release. You are strengthened when your energy is building and then released at the right moment. You are weakened when you block your energy or scatter your energy when it is meant to be released to flow freely.

The first thing you have to do when you feel this energy shift is direct your energy.

L. How do we direct our energy? Doesn't it just go where it goes?

G. No. Remember that **YOU** are in charge of your body. **YOU** are in charge of your mental body, your emotional body, your spiritual body, and your physical body. You are in charge of your life. It is your life, after all. You direct your energy. You keep your energy flowing freely or you block or scatter your energy.

L. That takes us back to my weekend with the tennis team.

Martina's energy was blocked. She felt like she was sick. She could hardly walk straight, much less run. Her stomach was carrying all the blocked energy. She did hurt.

G. This is a good example of fear in moments of opportunity. What were Martina's thoughts? That is where the blockage came from.

L. She was putting pressure on herself to win. She felt she had to win to prove herself. She has a goal of playing on the pro tennis tour. But her dad said that she wasn't good enough, and she believed him. Worse yet, she doubted her own worth. She doubted herself. She didn't know why she was playing. If she lost, she was "no good." If she won, well, she was "supposed" to win. Talk about a "no win" situation. No wonder she felt fear.

G. Her thoughts created the blockage, not her dad. Each of you is responsible for your own life. Each of you is in charge of your own life. No one else is in charge of you. Remember, this is your life, and you are in charge. You choose in each and every moment what is right and good for you. You choose what frees your energy. You choose what blocks your energy. You choose what scatters your energy.

Martina chose doubt. She chose to doubt not just her ability but herself. That is why she felt sick.

L. I can see that. It is so much easier looking at what is happening from an energy perspective. It is clearer. Thank you for the insight!

Highlights

1. Fear, as an emotion, is a thought linked with a sensation in the body.

2. Incorrect use of fear is energy that is blocked or scattered.

3. Fear triggers your body's inner security system.

4. Your body is a system of energy and information.

5. In moments of opportunity, your energy shifts, making you feel uncomfortable.

6. The first thing you need to do when your energy begins to shift is direct your energy.

7. The information you apply to your energy determines whether or not your energy is depleted or enhanced.

8. Your thoughts direct your energy.

9

Soaring with Your Body

L. Why does this happen to me? I feel all this energy before I get the computer out. I feel these questions forming and answers coming. Then when I face this empty page, I am not sure where we should start or even of what we have already covered. I am also afraid that this material is going to be difficult for people to follow. It seems so random. I'm not following my outline. In fact, I no longer have an outline. I feel a bit out of control.

G. Well, isn't that appropriate? We were talking about fear, weren't we? You may have observed that what you focus on expands. We've been focusing on fear. Thus you began to move into fear yourself. You are doubting your information.

L. No! That's not it! I don't doubt the information. I know that it is true. I have my own experience to verify that, not to mention the people who have been working with me. Is this energy stuff new?

G. Not new, really. But people's consciousness, their awareness, is continually deepening. You are opening up to more of who you are. Just as it takes time to know all the intricacies and fine lines of a beautiful work of art, it takes time to know yourself. You are a beautiful work of art! One of my most wondrous creations. Believe me, the more you know of yourself, the deeper you go, the more beauty you will find.

L. Oh, I don't know about that. People seem to be afraid to delve deeper into who they are. They seem to feel that the deeper they go, the more demons, the more ugliness, they will find.

G. It is necessary to get through the fear.

L. Oh, I should have known. We are back to fear. Fear is quite the topic. Most people don't even want to think about it.

G. Maybe they don't want to think about it or admit they are afraid, but they certainly live their lives in fear.

L. Okay! I'm ready. Let's get back into fear.

G. Linda, you don't have to go into fear to talk about fear. You learned that a couple weeks ago when you spoke at that international symposium on Hilton Head Island. You talked about fear. But you came from a place of love. That is why people could hear you.

L. Thank you. You're right, I was in fear earlier. It was blocking my energy. I couldn't open up to the information.

G. What were you thinking?

L. I started thinking, "What are people going to think about what I am writing?" "Am I making myself clear?" "Is this worth doing?" "What if people don't like what I have to say?"

G. Can you see how important what you are thinking is? This brings us to an important question: "How do you move into fear?" or "Where does fear come from?"

74

Let's get back to your tennis player, Martina. You said she was feeling a lot of pressure to win. She didn't believe in herself . . . When you asked her to tell you exactly what she was thinking, what did she tell you?

L. She said, "I'm not good enough. What's the sense of playing if I'm not going to be able to make it on the pro tour? If I can't win here, I'll never be able to win there. My father said I'm not good enough. The way I play, I'd never make it on the tour." I can't remember exactly everything she was thinking, but it was all along those lines. It's ironic. She is very good. She has great court sense, when she is not in fear, that is. She takes the ball early. She likes to take the ball in the air when she can. If she could dissolve the fear, the energy that is blocked, her body would explode, her game would skyrocket. You should have seen her returns. They blew me away.

G. I did see them. And you are right. It is fear holding her back, not any lack of talent. She is meant to play tennis. It is her mission. For now, keep working with her. You can help her to unleash her potential.

L. Thank you. I want to. I will! As long as she is open to me. Sometimes I think athletes think I am just giving them a pep talk.

G. That's because the energy to do what you suggest is inherent in what you tell them. It feels as if you are motivating them. It is a new experience to be motivated, inspired, and given the correct tools to accomplish something all at the same time. It is your gift. You help people shift their energy as well as teach them how to do it themselves.

But we are all one. We all need each other.

None of us is an island. None of us is alone. No one does it alone. We are meant to help each other. It is the best part of the system. I am always with you, even when you aren't aware of my presence. I am with you. Learning to welcome my love, as well as all love, will help you move out of fear. The antidote for fear is love. See the love inherent in the fear. Fear is love disguised.

L. I think we'd better talk about this. Love gets a pretty bad rap.

G. That's because love, just like fear, is not understood. The power of fear is underestimated. The power of love is even more underestimated.

L. I think people think of the power of love as some kind of lovey-dovey poetry kind of thing.

G. Au contraire. Never, never, NEVER, NEVER, NEVER UNDERESTIMATE THE POWER OF LOVE! NEVER!

L. Hmmm, are we talking about fear or about love?

G. Are they not the same?

L. Here we go again. Fear is love disguised, right?

G. Right! Just as you use doubt at the wrong times, you use fear when love works better, much better!

L. That takes us back to Martina. She was using the wrong fuel. Everything she was thinking was adding to her fear. She was fueling her emotional body with thoughts that blocked her energy. Naturally she felt awful. And of course it was tough for her body to move as it knows how to move. Much less at the level she wants to achieve.

G. That's right! You are in charge of your mental body. You choose your thoughts.

The thoughts you choose determine the tools you draw from inside of you. Your inner tools.

    Through the use of your breath and your thoughts you activate the inner tools you have at your command.

L. I have noticed from working with athletes that their problems have very little to do with their physical know-how. It is more with how to get their engines going. (If I can use that analogy to refer to the human body?)

G. Of course you can. It is a good one. It helps people to understand what you are saying. Your energy has to build and shift in order for you to perform at higher levels. That is when you need to program and guide your energy with the right information. The information that will allow your energy to gather and then to release at the right moment. To perform at a high level, you need more energy than to sit and watch TV for instance.

L. And that is where Martina went down the wrong track. She used information that blocked her energy.

G. Yes! And it is more complicated than that. Her intention was to play tennis at a high level. She was giving her body mixed signals. Mixed messages. So of course her body didn't know what to do. It would start out in one direction, only to be yanked back and on to another path. That kind of treatment is very hard on the body. It causes energy to be built up without a clear command as to the direction of its release.

Mixed messages cause stress in the body. Physically, it can cause dis-ease.

L. In Martina's case, it did cause quite a disturbance in her body. She felt ill. I didn't know whether she would even be able to play.

G. How did you help her?

L. Well, first I talked to her, asking her what she was feeling. At first she said she didn't know. She just didn't feel good. I told her I didn't think she was sick, but that it was the pressure she was feeling about her match. She agreed. Then I asked her how she felt about tennis. We had a long discussion about how she wanted to turn pro but now didn't think she was good enough. That she didn't know why she was playing anymore. I asked her if she wanted to play professionally. She said, "Of course, but I'm not good enough." I told her that she was right, that right now she wasn't good enough. But if she really wanted to play, she could. She could work on her game. She could learn how to play from love rather than fear. That is why I asked her, also, whether she really loves tennis. Whether she feels she belongs there, whether it is what she was meant to be doing. She said, "Yes," but still she was unsure of herself. I told her that too many people drop their dreams when they are challenged. And that is exactly when they can strengthen themselves and move closer to them. I also talked about the process, the playing of the game, and how that is what is important—not the winning or losing. Focusing on winning would only take her out of the moment, thus making it harder to win.

G. Did she understand what you were teaching her?

L. She seemed to. She then asked me what she needed to do. That was the hard part. It is so easy that people seem to underestimate its power.

G. How true that is! So what did you tell her to do?

L. I told her that it is through her breathing and her self-talk that she can start her engine, move it up a gear, keep it going at high levels, and enjoy the whole process.

G. Did she believe she could enjoy the process? How did she respond to that?

L. I don't think she believed me. She wanted to, but she has been programmed to believe otherwise.

G. So what happened? Did she play?

L. Yes, she played. First I told her how to start her engine (her physical body). I told her to start telling herself how much she loved playing tennis, that she was ready, that she was confident, that she was strong. I also told her to tell herself that she was safe, secure, and most of all that she was loved. Not to just mouth the words but to put feeling into the words. To believe them because they were true.

Confidence is a tool we all have at our disposal, a tool we can use to achieve success. That is how confidence is meant to be used, as a tool. Not the other way around. That is what most people do. They use success to achieve confidence.

It is backward to use success to achieve confidence, when confidence is the tool meant to achieve success!

G. Very good. Well stated! I couldn't have said it better myself!

Confidence is meant to be used to achieve your goals. And, more important, to fulfill your mission, your reason for being.

Confidence is often confused with competence. Competence comes from practice, from training, from experience. The more experience you have, the more competent you can become. It is the same for confidence. The more you practice confidence, the more you train confidence, the more experience you have with confidence, the more competent you become using confidence.

You, Linda, know confidence quite well. You know what it feels like. You know how to access it at will. That is part of what you are teaching the people who work with you.

Learning how to access all your inner tools is how you will learn to be at peace in your body.

Go on, tell us what happened with Martina. Don't leave your friends hanging. They want to know whether she was able to move through the fear. Did she play? What happened?

L. Let me start with Friday's matches, before we had a chance to work on what was blocking her energy. She won her first match, playing off and on with confidence. When she used confidence she played very well. When she didn't use confidence and used doubt instead, she didn't play well at all. Depending on which tool she used, she looked like a different person out there. With doubt, she did not appreciate her body's efforts. She hardly ever smiled. Especially in the second match. During that match, she won the first set 7–5. But she was struggling with herself the whole time. She was also pretty weak from not being able to eat. She didn't have much fuel to go on.

G. Not just food, she was fueling her body with negative thoughts. Remember that thoughts are fuel, just as food is. And thoughts are even more powerful than food as far as the effect they have on your body. Not that food isn't important. So, not only did she not have enough good food in her, but she also was pouring in mental fuel that drained her energy even more.

L. It was pretty tough to watch. I could see her energy getting weaker and weaker. She just couldn't pull herself out of it. Why couldn't I help her more? That's why I was there.

G. You can only help someone who is willing to help themselves. You can't do it for her. It is her body. She is the one in charge. You can guide her. You can help her. And if she is open and willing to change her energy, you can be of great assistance at that point. But Martina was low on fuel. She was tired. She didn't yet believe she could do it. So what happened then?

L. I stayed with her a little longer, but it became apparent there was nothing more I could do. I left to go to another match. She ended up losing that match in three sets. That night she was still feeling pretty awful. I told her that I would do a process with her the next morning if she wanted me to. She did. We were fortunate to have a rain delay on Saturday, giving me time to do a healing process with her before her first match. I helped her to move the energy that was blocked in her stomach area. She felt better. Then I repeated over and over again the script she was to follow with her thoughts. We called it a script because she could plan ahead of time which thought patterns to use during the match.

G. Very good. It is exactly like that. Just as she knows which outer tools she is going to use— her racquets, balls, and so forth—she needs to know ahead of time which inner tools she will use and how to access them. It's pretty easy with her racquets. They are in her bag. She opens up the bag and takes them out. Your inner tools can be accessed just as easily, once you know where they are and which key brings them out. That is the script you are referring to. Tell us exactly what you told her to do.

L. Okay. First we discussed what she needed to do before the match in order to "start her engine" and "get it warmed up." I told her what I said earlier about repeating with feeling, "I love tennis, I am ready to play, I love competition, I am strong, I am confident." Then I told her that she needed to take care of her body during the match. That she needed to give it clear instructions. And that she needed to nurture her body through the whole match if she wanted to raise her level of performance. After every point she was to follow the script. If she lost the point, she was to encourage her body by saying something like, "That's okay, we'll get it next time" or "That's okay, just move your feet faster." Whatever the correction, it was to be given with encouragement and love. I told her to smile and, if she could, even to laugh once in awhile. The more fun she could have, the better she would play.

G. Excellent! But didn't she have trouble with telling her body it was okay after she lost a point? After all, I'm sure she wasn't okay.

L. **The encouragement and statement of it being okay are not directed at the result but at her body.**

"That's okay" is meant to let your body know that you believe in it, that you are still there for it. That you aren't going to abandon your body just because of an error or a mistake. Instead, you are going to give it clear instructions as to how to do it better next time. That's the correction I talk about.

G. Very good, Linda! You have it! That is how to move the body to higher and higher levels. You really have no idea of what your body can do once you learn how to access your inner tools. And how to use all of you! It is very exciting, isn't it?

L. Oh yes! It is quite a sight to behold. The body blossoming, exploding before our eyes. And when it is your own body, what a treat that is!

G. Your body is meant to feel good. It is meant to be a joy. You can experience things in the physical body that you can't in spirit. But if you continue to come from fear in moments of opportunity, you will never experience the body as the beautiful creation it is. What did you tell Martina to do after she won a point?

L. It's funny, but even that was hard for her to do. Sometimes, she would respond so negatively that you'd think she had lost the point. She certainly wasn't having any fun playing. Imagine that, no fun playing! Are you sure we are supposed to be enjoying this experience down here?

G. How do you know that you are "down there?" Just kidding, we can get into that another time. To answer your question—yes, you are meant to have fun down there!

L. Good! There seems to be some confusion about that. So I told her that if she won the point, she must anchor it in by saying something affirming, like "Good shot," or "That's the way to do it," or "Beautiful." Anything that showed appreciation and affirmation for the job well done. Again, I told her to smile or even to laugh, that her body would feel better, and recover quicker if she did.

Oh, I almost forgot. I told her to take a deep breath immediately after the ball went out of play. Before she started thinking any thoughts that wouldn't enhance her performance. I want her to get used to taking care of her body after every shot. To be concerned with her body's welfare rather than the score. I believe this is how she will learn to stay in the moment, the present moment.

G. You are doing fine work, Linda.

L. Thank you! This is fun! I want to tell you that I feel great when you let me know that I am on the right track and that the work I am doing is in tune with you.

G. Of course it is! That's why you have so much energy doing it. It energizes you. You feel better after working with someone, no matter how difficult the topic, don't you?

L. Yes, I do. It's amazing. Yesterday, I had a session with another client. We talked, and then I did a healing and hypnosis session with him. When we were finished, I felt like my insides were cleaned out and massaged. I could feel my energy flowing freely through my body. It is the best feeling. I went on a long walk with Pam after that. I was noticing all the incredible fall colors. The sky was that blue that only seems to happen in Minnesota. And the air was fresh and crisp. I knew I was in heaven on earth. I could see the signs all around me. It took my breath away. Yes, I am definitely energized by the work I do.

G. Wonderful! Now, let's get back to your coaching. How did Martina respond to your suggestions?

L. Well, you'd think it would be easy enough to do. I mean, how hard is it to take care of yourself? It feels so much better than not taking care of yourself. But it wasn't easy for her. Well, let me tell you what happened in her match on Saturday.

She was on the court below me, so I could watch and see clearly everything that was going on. Her opponent was a fine player. A hard hitter. Full of power! Well, Martina came out there as if she had forgotten everything we had worked on. She wasn't using the script we had planned. She was definitely not taking care of herself. It was not a pretty sight to behold. She had no power behind her shots. No strength. Her opponent was good, very good. But I knew Martina could give her a better match if she followed our script. Her body didn't have a chance otherwise. She looked weak and ineffective. Yet I could see all this potential inside of her just begging to be allowed expression.

G. What did you do? Surely you didn't just let her spiral down that path of disappointment, did you? After all, that is what college coaching is about. You're supposed to help and guide your athletes in the right direction. This is one way people learn about helping and supporting each other, that all of us are one. You need to live your own lives, but you still need each other.

L. You're right. She did need help. She lost the first three games rather quickly On the changeover, I went down to the court to talk to her. I told her that if she didn't change something right away she would be back at the hotel, packing her bags, and on the next plane out of here so fast she wouldn't know what happened. I asked her whether she wanted to experiment. She had nothing to lose. I asked her to play the way we had planned.

G. And what did she say to that?

L. Well, she didn't really say much. But I took her response, as weak as it was, as a yes.

G. What exactly did you tell her to do then?

L. Just what we have been talking about. I'll pretend I'm talking to her now: "Martina, take a deep breath as soon as the ball goes out of play. Release the air slowly. Take another deep breath. If you win the point, say something encouraging to your body, anchoring in the shot. If you lose, say 'That's okay,' and give your body some kind of instruction as to how it can do it better next time. *Take care of your body after every point.* Forget about the score and who is winning or losing. *Your job is to feel good out there.* The more fun you can have the better. Let your body do what it knows how to do. Before you start each point, whether you are serving or returning, be sure you are ready. You are feeling strong and confident. Confidence is the tool you are going to use. So to draw confidence out, repeat with feeling, before you begin the point, 'I am strong. I am confident. I love tennis. This is fun!'"

G. You just have to repeat those affirmations and confidence appears?

L. You have to repeat them with feeling. With belief. That's the key ingredient, belief. You have to create the feeling of belief and the feeling of confidence. It's really quite easy, you know.

G. Yes, I do. The feeling is what it is all about. And so what did our Miss Martina do? Did she follow your instructions?

L. Yes! And it was quite amazing to see. On the return of serve, she was ripping back her shots. It was as if a totally new athlete were playing. As if I had done a substitution, like they do in basketball. Only, it was the same person.

G. Not really. It was a different Martina who went out there. It was a Martina who took care of her body. It was a Martina who knew how to draw out the inner tools that she has at her disposal. It was a Martina who felt good about her body and what her body could do. It was a Martina who appreciated her body's talent. Indeed, it was a different person! So how did she do? You know we all want to know how it turned out. Did she win?

L. Are you serious? You know it isn't about the winning or losing. You're pulling my leg!

G. Yes, I am pulling your leg, as you say. But I know your readers, and they still want to know whether she won or lost. They still think that her winning would justify what you told her.

L. The winning doesn't justify it. How can I get it across to athletes that it is about the process, the journey?

The end of the game is just one more moment in time to be experienced. No more important, or less important, than any other moment.

G. You just did. *Games are meant to reflect life.* Unfortunately, right now, having is more important to people than being. Thus athletes reflect life in that having the "win" is what is important. "Winning is having." "Losing is not having." It is that simple. Of course, that makes for a lousy life. "Having" wears off very quickly. And you're back where you started, needing to "have" again. It is a vicious circle. I don't think it's much fun, do you?

L. No, I don't. People look at me like I am crazy when I say you can feel good after a win or a loss. That you can feel happy and excited to play again, win or lose. How do I teach that? I haven't come up with the right words.

G. Learning to live from love in each and every moment is how you do it. The end of a match is simply another moment to live in love. Is beating yourself up with anger, blame, excuses, and frustration living that moment in love? I don't think so. Every moment, come from love. EVERY MOMENT! Then you will know life in the body as you are meant to live it. How much clearer can I be?

L. Well, that's pretty clear. Yet we do seem to have problems doing that. We don't know how to do it, or we would. Some moments we are taught how to come from love. But in many cases, we are taught that fear works better.

G. And does fear work better? Does lack of belief, anger, frustration, and impatience work better than confidence, belief, trust, joy, patience, and determination? No, of course not. You have been taught to come from fear in so very many situations. Remember that love is always the answer. And that is why we are writing this book. To give you the "how to" in easy to read instructions. So back to Martina. What happened?

L. She lost the first two points. But she followed the instructions, she took care of herself after each point, win or lose. Her body started to explode. She was now running faster, stronger. Her court sense was incredible! It was as if she knew where the ball was going even before it was hit. And she knew where to hit the ball. She set up the points like a master. She even smiled a couple of times. Once—it was so funny—this smile crept up on her almost without her knowing it was coming. She looked over at me, and there it was, a SMILE! She had to smile back at herself. It felt so good. Now, we had a match on our hands. They battled back and forth. Great points. I could see Martina growing in strength with each point, her opponent moving into frustration. But never giving up. She was a strong opponent.

G. Well, what happened?

L. You are so funny! You know what happened! She won the next six games to win the first set 6–3! On the crossover, she sat down next to me and said, "Whew, six games in a row!"

G. Oh, oh! What did that signal? She obviously was pleased with her first set.

L. Yes, she was! But the match was nowhere near over. She had to win another set.

G. What did you tell her? How was she doing?

L. She wanted it to be over at that moment. I don't think she knew whether or not she could keep playing at that level. She still didn't trust the whole process. She didn't realize that if she kept taking care of herself after every point, she would have the energy to play the whole match at that level and even higher. She had gone into fear. It happened so quickly that I almost missed it. I told her to keep doing what she had been doing.

G. And did she? Did she keep nurturing herself after every point as she had in the previous six games?

L. No, she didn't. I didn't understand at the time what was going on. Why she had reverted back to her old script. Especially when this one had worked so well.

G. What do you mean? Had worked so well?

L. She was winning!

G. Caught you! It isn't about the winning! Isn't that what you just said, not too long ago? It isn't about the winning or the losing. It is about the journey, the process. It is about feeling good, coming from love, in each and every moment.

L. You know what I meant! So, why did she revert back to fear? I thought she was feeling good.

G. Yes, she was beginning to feel good. But she still didn't trust the feeling. After all, she was used to feeling pretty awful when she played. And she had a lot of success while feeling awful. She had gotten very little feedback that it was supposed to feel good. Feeling good, in fact, was scaring her. She began to put all sorts of opinions on what she was feeling. She began to question it. Impatience crept in. Her chief feature!

L. What?

G. Her chief feature! We'll talk about that later! Back to Martina. What happened in the second set?

L. Well, she wanted the match to be over. I can see it now. She was afraid she didn't have the energy to stay at that level, much less go to a higher level. So she wanted it over before she ran out of energy. And, of course, the first game had to be a long, tough one. Back and forth they went. Over and over again. It was the longest game of the match. She ended up winning the game. But it took a lot out of her. And she wasn't running the script. She was in fear. I have no doubt of that now. I told her to keep doing the script. But she didn't seem to be listening as she had during the previous six games. I know now that since she was in fear I could have helped her better by addressing the fear. By putting it out in the open. In the light we could have dissolved it.

G. Very good. You have remembered something that is very important.

Take care of the fear, and the love will take care of the details.

L. I felt like I had done all I could. Now it was up to her. I knew that if she went to action, she could get back on track.

G. Of course. That is how you move out of impatience. You get something done. You move to action. Did she move to action?

L. Oh yes, indeed. She lost the second set, not being able to get back into it soon enough. I didn't know how she would play the third set. I just knew that this was a moment of opportunity for her. Would she take it, or would she refuse? To my delight, she took it. She played with joy that third set. She took care of herself after every point. She was determined! She chose the role of the warrior athlete! It was a great sight to behold.

G. I imagine it was. What happened to her opponent?

L. She played very well. But she couldn't raise her level of performance to match Martina's level. That was the difference. Martina went to another level.

G. Well, I guess we know who won!

L. Yes, Martina won! I was happy she won.

G. Were you, now? Are you sure it was because she won? Or could it have been that you were happy for her? For the process she went through. For the joy she began expressing in the last couple of games. Happy for the moment you shared with her and all the other people watching the match.

L.   Hmmm! I did feel good. Now that I think about it, that was because of the process, the joy that I felt when she was playing those last few games. I was proud of her for staying with it. For going through her fear. It wouldn't have mattered if she had won or lost. Although I have to admit that, at the time, I wanted her to win. And I was glad when she did.

G.   Of course you were. The object of the game is to win. And so you do get a feeling of accomplishment when you win at a sport or game. You are supposed to enjoy the winning, just as you can enjoy the losing.

L.   What? Oh please, I don't think I totally get it. And I can't explain that to these athletes. They think they have failed when they lose. And they have, haven't they? I mean if the object of the game is to win, doesn't it follow that if you lose, you have failed?

G.   No, you can't explain it. But I can! What is wrong with failing? Is that so bad?

L.   Well yes! Isn't it?

G.   Could it be your interpretation of failure that makes it so bad?

L.   Keep going. I think I'm beginning to see it again.

G.   Failure is just the other side of the coin. The way the game is set up is someone wins, someone loses. Is the better person the winner or the loser? No! Your worth does not change with the winning or losing. Do you have any control over who wins and who loses?

L.   Well, sure! If you play better than the other person, you win.

G. So why don't you win every time?

L. I see what you're getting at. It wouldn't be much of a game if we knew who was going to win. Or even if we could guarantee who the winner would be. Why play the game? Right?

G. Yes! Remember, sports and games are a joyful way to see how life is played. To learn how to use all the tools you have within you. Actually, no one ever loses. Do you remember me telling you that it is about love? About living each and every moment from love.

L. That sounds so weird, sometimes. I mean, to tell you the truth, I kind of like to get angry sometimes, even to feel sadness.

G. And losing? Do you like to lose sometimes?

L. No! I can't say that I like to lose. Now I am confused.

G. And do you like to be confused sometimes, too?

L. Okay! What are you getting at here?

G. What am I getting at, indeed? You tell me!

L. I can feel it forming within me. I almost have the answer. I just can't quite get it. I know it is there.

G. Keep going. Be not afraid. You do know. Be confused no longer. Be clear, LeClaire, be clear.

L. You sound like Charlie, now.

G. Another wise friend of yours!

L. Yes! When Martina won, that was the moment we were experiencing and so of course that felt better than losing because losing wasn't the moment we were in.

G. And if she had lost? Let's play out that scenario.

L. I would have been disappointed.

G. And would that have been so bad? Is disappointment such an evil feeling?

L. Oh, I get it! Of course! There is a place for disappointment. When disappointment is the appropriate tool for the situation.

Highlights

1. The thoughts you choose determine the inner tools you use.

2. Thoughts are fuel, just as food is fuel.

3. Nurture your body with higher-level thoughts as well as with healthy food.

4. Your energy has to build and shift in order for you to perform at higher levels.

5. Mixed messages to the body cause stress.

6. Choose inner tools just as you choose physical tools.

7. Confidence is a tool meant to be used to achieve success.

8. Competence comes from practice, from training and experience.

9. You need to practice confidence to be competent at it.

10. Play from love rather than fear.

11. Sport is meant to show you in a joyful way how life is played.

10

You Are a Creative Being

L. Let me get a cup of coffee before we start.

G. We have started already. You have lots of questions today. We left off at a pretty interesting place yesterday. And how did your day go after we stopped?

L. It was great. I got the garage cleaned out. At least cleaned out good enough for Josh to get his car in it again. I paid my bills. I went to the bank and the post office. I went for a long, glorious walk in the woods with Pam. I talked to Josh. I did some research. I talked to Bryce. Do you want me to go on?

G. You did quite a bit. How was your energy level?

L. I had all the energy I needed and more. I felt great. Well, except for . . .

G. Yes? Except for when?

L. Except for when I was talking to Bryce. That didn't go as well as I would have liked.

G. And who is Bryce?

L. My friend. I don't really want to bring him into this. He is a very private person.

G. Okay. Let's just talk about you! How did you feel as you went through the rest of your day and evening?

L. Like I said, I felt great. I was full of energy. Centered. Excited about what I was doing. Until I talked to my friend. Then my energy dropped.

G. Why? What do you think happened?

L. Well, we were talking about what he was doing. He was very excited about meeting three people who had won the Nobel Peace Prize. There was a reception for them where he had the opportunity to meet and chat with them.

G. That all sounds very nice. When did it start draining your energy?

L. There was so much that I wanted to know about them. And Bryce was only talking about what he was interested in. When I started asking him questions I was interested in, he started withdrawing his energy. He responded as if I was interrogating him. He no longer was in the same space.

G. He wanted to be in control of what he shared with you?

L. It would seem so. It is draining to talk to someone who doesn't share freely.

G. And does he have to share freely? Does he not have the right to share what he wishes?

L. Yes, of course! But why bother telling me anything if he doesn't really think I am interested. It seems pretty one-sided. I just get tired of the whole process. He awakens interest in me. Then as soon as I express interest, he withdraws his energy, as if it is so hard to "remember everything."

G. You were frustrated?

L. Yes, I was! Okay, so I know I wasn't very loving. I wasn't coming from love! But geez, it was frustrating! I didn't like my energy being drained from me like that. After all, he is my friend!

G. Now you sound a little angry? Perhaps?

L. Well, the more I think about it, the angrier I do get.

G. And why do you get angrier?

L. What do you mean, why do I get angrier?

G. He isn't doing anything (as you say) to you now. Why are you getting angry now? And, in fact, angrier?

L. You know this isn't what I want to talk about. What does any of this have to do with this book?

G. You mean this book about how to be at peace in the body?

L. Yes, that book! What has my conversation with Bryce have to do with what we are writing about?

G. You are kidding? Did you think this was just going to be an academic question? You didn't really think that you wouldn't be brought into the mix, did you? When have you ever not been a part of the process? This book is about you! And everyone who is drawn to reading it. We haven't just been talking about Martina here. We're talking about you and you and you. All of you. So yes, your experience with your friend is pertinent to this book. Besides, your next book is about relationships.

L. What! My next book! What next book? I haven't even got this book finished! I don't even know how I will finish this book.

G. Slow down! You have been asking me about your next book. What it will be about.

L. I have?

G. Yes, you have. You haven't had the courage to bring it up here, yet. But when you are walking, when you are reflecting, you have asked me. I have heard you, of course. So I thought I would surprise you today. You said you like it when I surprise you. You also want to know how many books you are going to write.

L.   And I have been afraid to ask that question, too?

G.   May I suggest that it is not that you are afraid to ask the question but that you are afraid I will give you the answer.

L.   So I'm afraid to know how many books I am to write? Why would that scare me? You'd think it would give me some consolation to know.

G.   This is very interesting. It would not give you consolation. You would feel limited. Constricted. Is that all, you would ask? Or the opposite, is that all I am going to do with my time from now on is write? There are so many other things I want to do. I won't have time to write that much. And on and on you would go. And rightfully so. You are a creative being. Creating is what you are all about. You are creating yourself in each and every moment. And if you ever really believed that your story has already been written, why bother to write it yourself? In other words, why bother to create what has already been created.

L.   Wow! I'm following that. On the one hand, living in uncertainty is hard. On the other hand, living with certainty is impossible. It wouldn't be living. At least not living as the creative beings we are.

G.   Very good, Linda.

Uncertainty is where creation begins. Moments of opportunity are moments of uncertainty.

That is what makes them powerful! You get to create in moments of opportunity. In moments of uncertainty. Pretty exciting, *n'est-ce pas?*

L. *Oui! C'est extraordinaire!*

G. That reminds me of something I said to Martina before she played her third match on Saturday.

G. What did you say to her?

L. I asked her whether I could play the match for her!

G. What did she say?

L. No! She wanted to play it. I told her to have fun then. Or why play?

G. Is everything supposed to be fun?

L. Yes! Isn't that what you said?

G. Yes! Life is meant to be joyful.

L. So that's my point. It is supposed to be fun!

G. She does have free will, you know! She can make it whatever she wants. She can create how she wants it to be.

L. That is why I always ask people what they want. Then, depending on what they say, I help them move in that direction.

G. Always ask. It will make your work a lot easier. Ask often. People change their minds. Ask often. Keep up to date with them. Up to the moment. It is a good question for athletes to ask themselves, is it not?

L. Yes! It is so easy to forget. Why am I doing something? Is it to make myself miserable? Sometimes, it feels like that is what people are thinking. Isn't that crazy?

G. No, not really. Not if you have been taught the power of fear and violence instead of the power of love and joy.

L. I see what you mean.

G. Back to our conversation about you. You were getting frustrated and angrier by the moment not too long ago. What happened to the frustration and anger? Where did it go? You aren't frustrated or angry now.

L. No, I am not. We changed the subject.

G. Did we?

L. Yes, we started talking about . . .

G. About you and me and fun and joy. And we spoke about the meaning of life. We spoke about creating. We said you are meant to create yourself in each and every moment. And you feel better. Why do you feel better?

L. I'm centered. I am focusing on what I want. I feel like I am back on my path. My energy is flowing freely again. I feel myself moving forward. So what did happen to me with my friend?

G. You felt held back. You had a million questions. You were curious for many reasons, reasons you hadn't shared with him. He had no idea where you were coming from with your questions. You went into fear. That is when your energy drained from you. You were afraid to ask the questions you wanted to ask. You were afraid of his response or lack of response. It was the fear that drained your energy. Not Bryce. Yes, he played into it. Beautifully. But you had a choice as to how to respond to his fear. You didn't have to go into it.

L. So I could have created a different situation between us by choosing a different response. But why do I always have to be the one?

G. Which one?

L. The one who has to . . .

G. Has to what? Love? What a tough assignment! Linda, Linda, Linda!

L. I don't think I like the way you are saying my name.

G. And how am I saying it?

L. Like I did something wrong.

G. And did you?

L. I thought you said in your previous books that there was no right or wrong. That is just a judgment we put on it.

G. Would you like a review?

L. Please!

G. Okay! You have a choice. Always!

How you create and how you respond to the experiences in your creation is your choice.

Whether or not you understand that it is you who creates your life, you can see that it is how you respond and the attitude you choose that determines the next step in your life's story.

Highlights

1. You are a creative being.

2. Uncertainty is where creation begins.

3. Moments of opportunity are moments of uncertainty.

4. You are creating yourself in each and every moment.

5. Ask yourself why you are doing something.

6. You always have a choice.

7. Life is meant to be joyful.

8. Fear drains your energy, not people.

9. How you respond to challenges and situations in your life determines the next step in your story.

10. Choose wisely.

11

Emotion, Feeling, or Just a Memory?

L. People are opening up to heart energy. They are feeling their hearts opening up, and they don't know what to make of it.

G. Okay, let's get back to the emotional body. What would you like to know?

L. First of all, what is an emotion? And what is the difference between an emotion and a feeling? Are they the same? Can we choose our emotions? Or are they just random and totally out of our control?

G. Slow down! One question at a time! What is an emotion? It will help you to understand if you can think of yourself as having an emotional body, just as you have a physical body. For indeed, you do have an emotional body. Though you can't see it with the physical eye, you can certainly feel its existence. You can't see your mind or your spirit, either. Yet you know that they exist.

L. Yes! I can definitely feel it. I can feel its power. Some people think that emotions are irrational. Is that true? Are they irrational?

Emotion, Feeling, or Just a Memory?

G. I see you do have many questions. Back to your first question. Emotions are one part of the emotional body. The emotional body is the whole. An emotion is a piece or part of the whole. One emotion, such as anger or frustration, joy or love, makes up only one small piece of the picture. Of your emotional body.

L. What else is the emotional body made of?

G. Feelings!

L. Feelings? Aren't feelings the same as emotions?

G. No! The difference between an emotion and a feeling will help you understand the emotional body and your emotions. A feeling is a sensation in the body. There is no thought, just feeling. Pure feeling. An emotion is a thought coupled with a sensation in the body. Feelings cannot be defined easily with one word or two. Feelings give you valuable feedback. Information. Someone asking you what you are feeling is asking you to describe what is going on in your body. For people who are not used to tuning into and listening to their bodies, this can be a difficult question to answer. They will often tell you what they are thinking, not what they are feeling. Feelings cannot lie. They cannot be denied. Well, I guess you could deny them. But they don't go away if you pretend they are not there. If you pretend you aren't feeling anything. Even if you have learned to ignore your feelings and think you truly are feeling nothing, they still are there.

L. Is that what we mean when we talk about repressed feelings?

G. Yes! Remember we said that the emotional body needs full expression. Well, if these feelings and emotions are not allowed expression but are instead stifled or repressed or denied all together, they turn inward. They often affect the physical body, causing dis-ease in the body.

Learning to tune into your feelings is a powerful way to live in your body. Feelings are giving you constant feedback as to what you are doing, how you are living, where you are going, who you are. Feelings let you know whether you are in tune with your true essence, which of course is love!

L. This is getting a little complicated. Can you give us another perspective on feelings?

G. Okay! Let's look at feelings from an energy perspective. You, in your body, in your essential state, are a system of energy and information. Your feelings are expressions of energy. There are only feelings of:

1. energy flowing freely
2. energy that is blocked
3. energy that is scattered, going in all directions.

L. What does that mean? How does that help us? You said feelings give us feedback, direction in our lives. How?

G. Very simply. When your energy is flowing freely, you are moving ahead, going forward in your life. You are on the right track. Remember, by "right" I mean that the direction you are going will get you to where you want to go. The direction is following your intention. If, on the other hand, your energy is blocked, your "feelings" (feeling your energy as blocked, stopped, or something isn't right) are telling you to slow down, to wait, to stop all together. It is telling you to look at what you are doing. Your feeling is blocking you from moving forward because you are heading in the wrong direction.

L. So when our energy is blocked, it is blocked to help us. To keep us from moving in the "wrong" direction?

G. Yes! Once you change directions and get back on the right path, your energy is freed and flowing freely once again.

L. Oh, I get it! After you make a decision, when it is the right decision, you can feel a sense of relief.

G. Yes, exactly! That sense of relief is your energy being released to flow freely again. It feels good. Blocked energy is not meant to feel good. If it did, you would have no clue to change anything. That uncomfortable feeling is a valuable motivator for change!

L. But sometimes it keeps people from making changes. They "feel" as if they can't do anything.

G. That is only because they don't understand how their body is meant to function. They don't understand how to unblock the energy.

L. What happens when our energy is scattered?

G. It's almost the opposite. You are going in too many directions at once. You need to slow down and center yourself. Get more balanced. When your energy is scattered and going in all directions, you are in a weakened position. You start in one direction, only to switch paths at the first hint of trouble. Or you have lost your direction. You don't know where you are going, and so you first go one way, then change your mind and go another direction, and back and forth and so on and so on. Never getting anywhere, except exhausted!

L. That happens often in the business world. Someone will start one project and, when confronted with a challenge, move on to another project without finishing the first one. They have a lot of ideas but can't seem to follow through on any one of them. I also see this with athletes.

G. Yes, of course! It is another way athletes can teach us about life through their experience in competition. Watching athletes work with their bodies as an energy system can give you valuable insight. You can learn how to keep your energy flowing freely by watching an athlete do it. It's an interesting and fun way to learn about your body, wouldn't you say?

L. Yes! But so many athletes don't have a clue. Their energy gets blocked or scattered, and they don't know what to do. They aren't even aware of what their energy is doing. They just know they don't like how they are feeling. And they look for something on the outside to help them. Instead of looking on the inside.

G. Work with your energy, free it. Allow it to flow freely and your outside problems will take care of themselves.

L. I have an example of that happening with one of my athletes on the tennis team.

G. What happened?

L. Chris was playing her championship match at Notre Dame. It was the same weekend Martina was going through her stuff. Only with Chris, her energy was scattered, not blocked. She had lost the first set, 0–6, and was down in the second set, 0-3. As you know, in tennis you have to win two out of three sets. To win a set, you have to win six games, by two. So, now you can see that Chris was running out of time. Three more games and the match could be over. I had come over to her court just as she was starting the second set. As I watched her play, I could see that her energy was scattering all over the place. She was, indeed, lost. I sat down next to her at the changeover. It was 0–3. I asked her what was going on. Even though I could see how scattered her energy was, I wanted to know what she was aware of.

G.   And was she aware that her energy was scattered?

L.   No. At least, not aware in the sense that the awareness caused her to change the situation. When I asked her what she was feeling, she looked at me, hardly able to contain herself. Her energy was going all over the place. All she could do was laugh. She even said, "I can't help but laugh. I feel so weird. Like I don't know what is going on. I can't seem to hit the ball with any strength. And I have very little accuracy."

G.   The laughter was good for her. It helped her to redirect her energy.

L.   How did it do that?

G.   Laughter is a signal to the body of joy and healing. What did you say to Chris?

L.   I told her that her energy was scattered and that she just needed to get centered. I told her to take a deep breath. Several deep breaths. To turn her attention to her breathing. To focus on the breathing in and the breathing out.

G.   Very good. The breathing helped her to "gather" her energy. To bring her energy in. To give it direction once again. How did she respond?

L.   Great! She did what I told her to do. Then, I reminded her that this was supposed to be fun. That after every point she was to take care of her body. I told her what I told Martina to do.

G.   What did she say?

L. It was great. She said, "Getting mad and frustrated at myself isn't helping me." "That's right," I said. Then I told her that she might run out of time, but the score wasn't what was important here. What was important was that she learn how to get centered and back on the right track when her energy gets scattered.

G. So did she make a great comeback and win the match?

L. Yes and no! She made a great comeback, and she lost the match. She started hitting her shots. She broke serve three times before running out of time, losing the match, 0–6. 3–6.

G. And was she devastated?

L. For a few moments she was. I talked to her about how proud I was of her for being able to gather her energy and center herself in the middle of the match. She never gave up. She just didn't know what to do. We talked about how next time, she'll be aware sooner when her energy gets scattered. Then she can respond sooner, giving her more time. She liked that idea. I told her to express appreciation to her body for all the work it had done. She then told me that she could hardly lift her arm, it hurt so much. So of course I told her to get some care for her arm. And before I knew it she was talking about what is really important in her life. The winning, or rather the losing, moment was over. She was moving ahead. She was living. She was staying in the moment. Her face glowed. It felt so good sharing those moments. She moved out of disappointment so quickly. After getting some ice for her arm, she headed for another court, to cheer on her teammates.

G. How was she feeling the rest of the day?

L. She was happy. Laughing, talking with everyone. Her energy was flowing freely. She was light and free! She was filled with love.

G. That is the secret of healing, you know. Love! It got her energy moving freely. This story is a good example of how weak your energy gets when it is scattered all over the place, whether in sport or in life. Chris lost her direction. Her shots reflected that, going all over the place. She had forgotten her intention. That is why it is so good that you have the athletes write down their mission statements and read them to themselves before they play. It gives them the direction they need.

L. I don't think Chris had written her mission statement yet.

G. Probably not. She had lost herself for awhile. You helped guide her back to herself. That is the best thing you can do when someone's energy is scattered. This, of course, happens quite often to people in their lives. When people are faced with many opportunities or things to do, they get overwhelmed because they try to do everything at once. Not really doing anything well. You will feel weaker when your energy is scattered. That is why people feel like they can't do anything at all.

L. So, the antidote to scattered energy is to take one thing that you can do and do it.

G. That's right. That is what you helped Chris to do. She was trying to play the whole match in one point. And the more that didn't work, the more she kept trying to do it all at once. Not only was she trying to play the whole match at once, but her mind was off somewhere else, too. She was trying to do more than just play tennis. Her mental body went off to other places.

L. Which is why she was having trouble focusing. She was trying to focus on several things at once.

G. Right! Spot on! As they say in England!

L. So, getting back to the emotional body, where were we? Is this all connecting?

G. Yes, of course.

Feelings are expressions of energy.

We just demonstrated an example of someone whose energy was scattered and the effects on her body. Your feelings are always giving you valuable feedback. Chris felt uncomfortable. She knew that what she was doing wasn't working, but she didn't know what to do to change it. She was looking on the outside for help, when all she needed was inside of her. She had the tools to gather her energy and redirect it once again.

L. Okay, let's see if I can summarize what we have said so far.

1. **We have an emotional body, just as we have a physical body.**
2. **Emotions are just one part of the emotional body.**
3. **Feelings are another part of the emotional body**
4. **Feelings are different than emotions.**
   - **An emotion is a thought coupled with a sensation in the body.**
   - **A feeling is simply a sensation in the body. There is no thought attached to it.**

G. That is pretty good. There is more!

Emotion, Feeling, or Just a Memory?

L. I thought so. I certainly have more questions. But this is helping. I feel like it is getting clearer.

G. Now, isn't that an interesting thing to say. You "feel" like it is getting clearer. What do you mean by that? Describe what you are "feeling."

L. Well, it's kind of hard to explain.

G. Just describe what you are feeling, without any judgment or interpretation.

L. Okay. I feel this energy in my upper-chest area. More in my throat area, really. It feels like there is something blocked there, but it is getting unblocked, somehow. Like something is clearing it out. Almost like when you clear your throat physically. Only I know there isn't anything there. Except for energy, of course. The energy is still blocked in my throat, but not as much.

G. Now that is interesting! Your fifth chakra. The area of communication. Feelings are about communication. Feelings are your body's way of communicating with you. So it's not surprising that you are feeling energy in that area. How do you interpret that feeling?

L. That it is getting clearer. I am beginning to understand.

G. Good work. That is what it is communicating to you.

L. You said there was more. So far we have discussed the emotional body and how emotions and feelings are parts of the whole. Are there any more parts to the emotional body?

G. Oh yes, there are! The emotional body also has memory!

L. Memory?

G. Yup! Memory!

L. Wait a minute, God doesn't say "yup!"

113

G. What do you mean, "God doesn't say 'yup?'" How do you know what I say or don't say?

L. I've read the Bible. I went to religion classes for many years.

G. And they told you how I speak?

L. Yes!

G. And how do I speak?

L. You use words like "thou," blessed and holy words.

G. Holy words? You're pulling my leg again, aren't you?

L. No! I've been wondering about the choice of words you've been using. I didn't say anything before because it wasn't too bad. But "yup?" There isn't an English teacher in the world who would agree to "yup!"

G. What if this weren't in English?

L. What do you mean? Of course it is in English.

G. We'll see! Would you prefer I said something like "Thou has spoken the truth!" Does that sound better to you?

L. No! I guess "yup" is okay. It just sounded so funny to hear God say "yup!"

G. "Yup" sounds funny coming from anyone. It is a funny word. Can we get back to the emotional body?

L. Yes! Now, where were we?

G. You were asking about memory.

L. Oh yes, I remember!

G. Not that kind of memory! That is the memory of your mental body. Your mental body stores the memory of facts, of things that have happened to you. It stores the who, what, where, how, and even the why. The emotional body stores memories of emotions and your interpretation of what happened.

Emotion, Feeling, or Just a Memory?

L. This is getting interesting. Is this going to explain why all of a sudden an emotion is triggered in my body when I hear a song, or see a photo, or hear a story?

G. Yes! The emotional body stores the emotions you feel in any given situation. For instance, you hear "your song" on the radio. It transports you to a time when you were with this other person and you listened to the song together. You were in love, perhaps. You danced to the song, whispering sweet nothings in each other's ears. You were happy, joyful, confident, full of hope and excitement. These emotions are now released in the body, and for awhile you are living them all over again. This is a beautiful process. Especially when the emotions are such high-level ones as joy, happiness, and love. Because emotions are feelings coupled with thought, you also recall more details or memories of whom, what, and where.

L. Is that why we can remember so vividly some things from the past and others seem to be forgotten forever?

G. Yes! If you want to recall a moment filled with emotion, there are many triggers. As I said, you can hear a song that was playing only in the background of a dinner you were having. The song triggers the emotions you experienced at the dinner. A certain fragrance or aroma can trigger a memory stored in your emotional body.

L. That explains why I often remember what I was feeling during a speech I have heard. Sometimes I can't remember exactly what someone said, but I remember how I felt. Whether I felt good or not. I will describe someone from that feeling level. In fact, I prefer this kind of description of people, over the details of what they said. Maybe that is

what causes some of the distress in my conversations with
my friend. He speaks about the details of who, where, and
what. And I am interested in the emotional content of the
conversation or speech or whatever it is.

G. Are you just interested in the emotional content?

L. No! I want some of the details, too. I do need some of the
who, what, and where to satisfy my mental body.

G. That is perfect! Your mental body demands that kind of
information. It loves facts, ideas, thoughts. That kind of
thing.

L. Okay! So the emotional body has memory. Is there anything else we need to know about that?

G. Yes! If your emotions have not been expressed fully at the
source of their creation, they will be stored in your body in
repressed form. Waiting to get out.

L. What do you mean, "waiting to get out?"

G. Well, let's see. How can I best explain this? Maybe I need
to talk a little more about the nature of emotions. We have
talked quite a bit about "feelings" but not all that much
about emotions. Do you remember what I said earlier about
emotions?

L. Sure! You said that emotion fuels the physical body. Emotions can raise or lower the body's performance. Higher-
level emotions (patience, joy, confidence, for instance) raise
one's performance, while lower-level emotions (impatience, frustration, anger, and so on) lower it. The physical
body responds to the emotions we experience.

G. That's right. Here is another point, and this is important.
You *have* an emotional body. You are not your emotions.
When you are expressing an emotion, it seems you will
always feel that way.

Emotion, Feeling, or Just a Memory?

Inherent in emotion is the feeling that it will last forever.

It is all-encompassing. And emotion is always felt in the present. It feels as if it is happening right now, even if you are reacting to something that happened a long time ago.

L. How can we choose our emotions? How can we choose higher-level emotions? Don't emotions come and go at their own discretion?

G. You can choose emotions by the thoughts you hold. Remember, emotions are thoughts coupled with sensations in the body. You can choose your emotions by choosing your thoughts. You control your thoughts. You can choose your thoughts, your attitude, the way you respond to any situation. You can do it the other way around, too. You can create the sensation in your body first. When you smile before you feel like smiling, you feel better, if only for a brief moment. This can be less effective. Changing your thoughts works better. Sometimes, though, you just have to do it the other way around. This often happens when you "think" you are right.

L. And so you get stuck in a thought. The thought is what causes the problem. Is that right?

G. If you mean it blocks your energy, then yes. And because it blocks your energy, it keeps you from taking action or making a change.

L. I have another question. So often, it seems, we go in and out of emotions. Without any control. They just seem to happen to us. I think a lot of people would say that they can't help the way they feel. That something happens in

117

their lives, and they respond emotionally, without any say
as to the emotion they feel.

G. That isn't true. It may seem you have no say in which emotion you experience. But you do! You always have a choice
as to how you respond to any situation in your life.

L. But what about when I'm going through my day, one moment feeling great, the next moment feeling depressed, and
so on and on throughout the day?

G. Awareness! Thousands and thousands of thoughts go
through your mind and into your emotional body. You think
without awareness of your thoughts. It is similar to the
way many of you eat food. You put junk into your physical
bodies, chip after chip, for instance, without realizing how
much you are eating. You go through the day nibbling on
this and that, and before you know it, you have taken in
much more food than if you were aware of what you were
doing. Which is, of course, one reason that many of you
have a heavier body than is comfortable.

L. Because I am not aware of what I am thinking, my emotions go up and down without any obvious reason. So, I
interpret them as irrational or just coming from nowhere.

G. That's right. Which brings us back to one of your earlier
questions. Are emotions irrational? Never! There is always
a reason for the way you feel. In fact, your thoughts may
be "irrational." Because your mental body can think anything, it can think "irrationally" too. Unlike your emotional
body. Emotions are thoughts linked with sensations in the
body. If your thoughts deplete your energy, you experience an emotion in tune with that depletion of energy. On
the other hand, if your thoughts energize you, you experience emotions in tune with that energized feeling. Thus, if

you don't know why you feel a certain way, look to your thoughts.

L. Sometimes, I'm just thinking about someone and I feel my energy being depleted. How does that work?

G. Emotions are contagious! You can pick up the emotions of someone else simply by tuning into them, by thinking about them. Of course, this is more obvious when you are talking to someone. You begin to pick up on what they are thinking about, and it changes your energy.

L. Is this how someone can motivate someone else?

G. That's right! The person doing the motivating holds a certain thought that is coupled with the sensation in the body and holds this emotion with great intensity. The strength of the emotion, the energy, floods the person taking in the information. The information is in tune with the emotion the motivator wants to elicit from the recipient. For instance, if you want to fire up people, incite passion, come from a passionate place yourself. If you want to incite anger, use anger. Emotion begets emotion. Of course you don't have to respond to what someone is saying just because he or she wants you to. You can disagree with the thought being put out. If you have another thought, one that creates a different emotion, you will feel differently.

L. So let me get this straight. Emotions are contagious. But if we are aware of what we are thinking, or aware of what someone is saying, we can choose the emotions we desire.

G. That's right.

L. But I still don't get it. What about all those times when we just really can't help how we feel.

G. Remember, feelings are not the same as emotions. Feelings are your body's way of giving you information. Your body is taking in information all the time. Your intuition is a part of this system. It gives you constant guidance, feedback as to whether you are on the right track, as to whether you are in danger from an outside source. You don't want to control your feelings. They are always giving you valid information—information you can use and often need.

L. Give me an example, besides the danger one.

G. Okay. Someone tells you something. You have a reaction in your body, a "gut feeling" that the person is lying. That "feeling" gives you information that you may not be able to get any other way. Now, you may misread the feeling you have. Something may have been triggered in you by what was said, by a look that reminded you of someone or something that triggered an emotion stored in your body. But that is going into more depth than I want to in this book. Emotion is an interesting subject today because you are opening up to the heart energy that is coming into your awareness at this time.

L. That sounds like it could be a book about relationships.

G. And well it could be!

Highlights

1. Emotions are just one part of the emotional body.

2. An emotion is a thought combined with a sensation.

3. You have an emotional body, you are not your emotional body.

4. The emotional body has memory.

5. Unexpressed emotions are stored in your body.

6. Emotions raise or lower your performance.

7. You choose your emotions through your thoughts.

8. Your emotions are always rational; your thoughts may be irrational.

9. Lower-level emotions drain your energy while higher-level emotions enhance your energy.

10. Look to your thoughts to see why you are expressing a certain emotion.

11. Emotions are contagious.

12. A feeling is a sensation in the body.

13. Feelings give you constant feedback—they don't lie.

14. Feelings are about communication.

15. Feelings are expressions of energy—energy that is blocked, scattered, or flowing freely.

16. Laughter is a signal to the body of joy and healing.

17. The secret of healing is love.

12

Living Fully in the Flow

G. Hello, Linda! Did you have a nice day of recovery?

L. Hi! Yes! Is that what that was all about?

G. Balance, my dear Linda! We've only briefly talked of balance. But it is an important key to living peacefully in your body. Learning to flow with your energy is the easiest way to achieve balance. Do what feels right in the moment, and you can't go wrong. That's what you did yesterday.

L. It didn't turn out like I thought it was going to. But it was a wonderful day. I certainly have no regrets.

G. Tell us what you did. It can be a bit difficult going with the energy at first. Readers will appreciate an example of how you do it.

L. Okay! But it doesn't seem like much to me. On Sunday night I thought I would be writing on Monday morning as usual. I was excited about the work we have been doing. I was pretty tired Sunday night but still wanted to keep going. That was not to be. In fact, I didn't work on the book at all.

First of all, I woke up later than usual. Then I had to run some errands that needed to be done in the morning. At least that was where my energy felt it needed to go. Then when I got home, Josh was waiting at the door for me. He was home from college because he had the day off. He wanted to go out to lunch. Well, I'd never turn down an invitation for lunch with my son. We ended up having lunch and doing some errands together. It was a great time. Now that he's in college, we don't have much time alone together. So it was really good to have the time to talk with him and get caught up.

G. Which if you hadn't gone with the energy you would have missed out on.

L. How can people learn to go with the energy? To live each and every moment from their essence?

G. Well, you just gave the answer. Living from your essence in every moment is part of the trick. Of course it isn't really a trick. It's just how your body functions, how you were created. Which is what we've been talking about in this "manual." Coming from your core, from your essence, is how to live in your body.

L. Whenever you talk about "core" or "essence," it touches me at such a deep level. I can't even explain where the "feeling" comes from. I just know that it comes from a place deep, deep inside of me. I feel as if I do some sort of inner adjustment, and somehow I am back on track. I have a sense of mission. I know who I am. I know what I am all about. I am strong. I am confident. My energy is flowing freely. I feel great!

G. Yes, of course you do. Whenever you tune into your core, your essence, you are tuning into the strength, the knowing, the love that you are. You are supposed to feel great when you are being all that you are. It is when you are not coming from your essence that you don't feel so good.

L. This raises a ton of questions for me. Are we ever going to get it all down in this book?

G. No! Not in one book. Patience, my dear! All in the right time! This book is about the basics. Take these basic truths and build from them. When you know how your body, mind, heart, and spirit work, what they need to do, what they are meant to do at their optimum levels, you can take off. You can soar with the stars. You can reach the moon. You can fly like the wind.

L. That is what I want! So what are the steps to coming from one's essence? Let's get to the core of this question!

G. All right! To come from your essence in any moment, follow these simple guidelines:

1. **Awareness** (Be aware of your thoughts, your actions, your emotions, your energy, and your intention!)

2. **Flexibility** (Be willing to change your plans, to make plans and change them at a moment's notice.)

3. **Desire** (Want to come from who you are, from the depths of your soul.)

4. **Knowledge** (Know thyself! Who are you? If you can't answer simple questions like, "Who are you?" "Why are you here?" "What is important to you?" and "What do you want?" you don't know yourself and you will find it impossible to come from your essence in each and every moment. How can you come from your essence if you don't know your essence?)

5. **Silence** (Cultivate silence to reflect, to hear your inner guidance, to know yourself. It is a great gift to yourself and others.)

L. How do you give silence to others?

G. It is a gift to sit in silence with someone. You hear people say that "people who pray together, stay together." Well, that's often what silence is. Prayer.

L. How is silence prayer?

G. In silence, I talk to you. You listen. Prayer is one of the ways I communicate with you.

L. I thought prayer was when we talked to you.

G. That is how many of you pray. But it is only one side of prayer. How are you ever going to hear the answer if you are always doing the talking?

L. Oh! I get your point!

G. Thank you! It's an important one.

Whether or not you believe in ME, you need silence to hear guidance.

L. Amen!

G. Amen!

L. So is that all we need to know to learn how to follow our flow?

G. That and practice and training. You must train yourself to follow these steps. Then you must practice them. Practice them often. In fact, make your life the practice of following these steps!

L. So, if I follow these five easy steps, I will learn how to be in the flow. All I have to do is: be aware of what I am doing, thinking, and feeling; be flexible; know who I am, want to be in the flow; and be silent often enough to hear the inner guidance at my disposal?

G. That's right.

L. But it should be more complicated than that.

G. Complicated, no! Do you think I cannot explain clearly and simply how you can live in peace, while in your body?

L. If it is so simple, why is it so hard for people to do?

G. It's not meant to be hard! Is there anything that I have said or suggested that you cannot do? That you are incapable of doing?

L. Well, not incapable, but it's difficult, that's for sure.

G. And why do you say difficult?

L. Because so many people have such a difficult time living their lives in peace. Even knowing what it means to live in peace.

G. Of course, which is why it is time for you to know more about your body system and how it is meant to live. Has there not been more and more information given to you about how you can be happier, more successful, and more peaceful? Why you, Pam Welter, Lorraine Moore, and Peggy Henrickson have written a wonderful book for children and young adults about how to be more peaceful. Your inner guidance has always been there for you. You just haven't known how to listen and hear it. I tell you, open to your own inner guidance and you will find a peace you have always known was possible.

Imagine, if you can, that life is really a game. A game where the object of the game is to find yourself. The real you. Not your body. You! And unbeknownst to you, you are lost in your body. All you have to do is find *yourself* in all the different situations and experiences in your life. And in order to find yourself, you have to know who you are. So you go out searching to find out who you are. You try out different roles and ways of being. Little by little you discover who you are, sometimes by finding out who you are not. You eliminate possibilities. Eventually, you reach a point where you know who you are, but you have lived out so many roles and programs that you then have to dismantle the programs that don't work, the programs that are not in tune with who you are.

L. This is starting to sound like life is supposed to be some sort of hardship. Trials and tribulations.

G. If you want it to be that way, yes. You can set it up any way that you want. It is not my intention that you suffer. Suffering is your creation.

L. But what about all the things that happen in life that cause us to hurt and suffer?

G. Such as?

L. This is so hard. I am afraid to even bring them up for discussion.

G. Why are you afraid?

L. Because of what you might say.

G. And what might I say?

L. That in all of life there is pain and loss.

G. You are speaking of death, perhaps?

L. Yes! Death! I don't know how to get around that. If anything happened to Josh, I don't know if I could stand it. Or to anyone I love.

G. How would you feel if Josh were to die today?

L. I don't even want to think about it, it hurts so much.

G. What hurts?

L. The loss.

G. Now we are talking about something all together different. We are no longer discussing the emotions. We are discussing the mental body, thoughts.

L. Go on, please.

G. You have thoughts that are hurting you. You are thinking that this person is lost to you forever. No! His form may change. But he can be with you, whenever you like. Remember when we discussed being flexible?

L. Yes! But this is being more than flexible. This is changing the truth.

G. The truth! And what is your truth?

L. Oh, I don't know. I don't want to talk about it anymore. There doesn't seem to be any answer.

G. Tell me, my dear child, are you coming from love now, or fear? Is this beautiful falling snow not putting you into a thought pattern of fear? Fear that your son will be travelling on dangerous roads?

L. Yes. But what can I do? I don't want to deny it. Yet I don't want to focus on it. What we fear we attract! That is what you said.

G. Linda, Linda, Linda. Is what you are thinking doing you any good?

L. No, it's not.

G. Then stop thinking it!

L. I can't!

G. Yes, you can. You do not create the lives of others. You can only create your own reality.

L. But how can I stop worrying about my son?

G. By stopping. If your thoughts do no good, if they do not lead you to where you want to go, why think them? You can instead choose discipline to guide your thoughts to where you want to go. Is it not quite beautiful when you look out your window at the falling snow?

L. Yes, but . . .

G. No! Not but! Enjoy your day! Make this day a day you are happy! Choose to be happy. Why choose to worry?

L. You are right.

G. Thank you!

L. It is what I am always preaching!

G. Practice what you preach!

L. Yes! Practice what I preach. Of course. Okay. Let's go over it again. How do I do that?

G. Oh, Linda. You do like to be clear! You know how to do it. Simply choose other thoughts. Choose appreciation, for example. Take a deep breath. You are not in charge of the universe. Death is a part of life as much as birth is. Death is no more the end than birth is the beginning. You are immortal, Josh is immortal, Lisa is immortal, Bryce is immortal, Pam is immortal, and all your family and friends are immortal. You never die! You simply change form. You leave your physical body. You will always have these people in your life. They are and always have been a part of you. Do you not feel today the presence of your father? After eighteen years?

L. Yes, I do. But that seems different.

G. On this question, Linda, I want you to know that I am with all of you. I know death is not easy. It is not easy because you do not know how to communicate freely with your loved ones who have left their physical bodies. You are learning more and more now about how to do that. It is the right time to open up to communication with all. I have blessed many of you with the knowledge and ability to openly communicate with people who have left their bodies. Many more of you are opening up to this communication and thus learning how to hear your loved ones' communication with you. We are all one, always! Death does not separate. It just changes things.

L. I want to believe that. I think any parent can understand my questions.

G. You mean your doubt. Go into love instead. Your choice in this matter is clear. You can worry your whole life about losing someone, or you can spend your whole life loving someone while they are in the form you recognize now. But I can tell you this, when someone you love changes form, you will be able to be with them and communicate with them if you want to. It is my promise to you. Believe, and it shall be done unto you. What more can I say about this subject?

L. When you put it that way I feel better. Yet I would bet there are people who don't want to die.

G. Are you so sure?

L. Well, no. But I don't hear people talking about wanting to die very often. Unless they are depressed, that is. And then they are really wanting to run away from their lives rather than wanting to die.

G. The desire to die is a desire to be with God. To be in love. You can experience me, you can experience love in your body. In fact, that is the reason you are in a body. To know love. To experience love. To express love in every moment, in every choice. In your body, you have a choice. You always have a choice. Don't you think it interesting to have the choice to come from love or not?

Living Fully in the Flow

L. Why would anyone not choose love?
G. Why indeed? Perhaps to know the other side.

Highlights

1. Learning to flow with your energy is the easiest way to achieve balance.

2. Live from your essence.

3. Come from your essence through: awareness, flexibility, desire, knowledge, and silence.

4. Prayer is one way God talks to you.

5. You are in a body to learn more about yourself.

6. Life is a game where the object of the game is to find yourself.

7. It is not life's intention that you suffer.

8. You can worry your whole life about losing someone or spend your whole life loving that person.

13

Traps

L. I don't feel so "good" today.

G. And why is that?

L. Well, I don't know.

G. "I don't know" is one of the best ways you have to stay in confusion. It is also another way you have to keep yourself from doing something.

L. All right, I do know. I just don't want to talk about it.

G. You don't want to talk about it, or you don't like the answers you are getting? Let's do a little exercise here. We have been talking about how to live in peace in the body. Let's practice what you have been learning.

L. I'd like that. I don't feel at peace right now.

G. The first step, we said, is awareness. You need to be aware of what you are thinking, feeling, and doing. Honesty is vital here. If you try to fool yourself, you will always lose. So what is going on with you?

L. I had a conversation with my friend again last night.

G. And how did it go?

L. I just felt so uncomfortable. Like there was so much he wasn't telling me.

G. Like what?

L. Like how he was feeling, for instance. He told me about talking to someone about going to see this doctor about diabetes. That he's been in the library reading and doing research about it. Then he told me about talking to two people over lunch about a job opportunity.

G. What disturbs you? It sounds like he was just sharing his day with you.

L. Well, yes, he was. But he was talking as if it were sunny all day and he played tennis. These are important issues he is dealing with. They concern me. They are a part of my life, too.

G. Do you trust him?

L. What do you mean, do I trust him? What has that got to do with anything?

G. You are obviously afraid of something, Linda. What is it?

L. This isn't about me. It is about him. If he could just share what is going on with him, I'd feel better.

G. It is about you. It is always about you. Living in a body is always about you. This is your life. This is your story. This is your creation. What are you creating?

L. How can this be about me? We were talking about him.

G. Okay, Linda, step back for a moment. This is about you. How are you creating this situation?

L. How am I creating it? What do you mean, me? I'm not creating it. This is about what is going on with my friend, not me!

G. That's where you lose your way. You asked me earlier about how people have lost their way. Whenever you go outside of yourself, you lose your way.

L. How do we "lose our way?"

G. Whenever you look outside of yourself, you are looking in the wrong place. In the wrong direction. You are in charge of your life. You have free will. You create your life. How you do that is about how you use your mental, emotional, physical, and spiritual body. What you choose to think. How you choose to respond to any situation in your life determines your next step, and your next step, and so on and so on until you have written a whole chapter. Before you know it, you have written the whole story. Your story.

L. How do we look within ourselves?

G. Honestly. By being totally honest with yourself. By knowing yourself so well that honesty is no longer a choice. It is something you do. It is as natural as breathing. You would no sooner be dishonest than you would stop breathing. That is how you stay on your path.

L. That sounds easy enough.

G. It is.

L. So why are we so dishonest with ourselves and others?

G. Fear. Whenever you move into fear, your thinking becomes unclear. You are in a position of weakness. And from this place of weakness, your decisions lead you farther and farther down the path of fear. This would be a good time to talk about chief features.

L. Yes! Every time I talk about chief features, it seems to give people a better understanding of what holds them back when they get close to achieving their goals, or even how to take the first steps toward their goals.

Maybe we should start out with a definition of chief feature. I am not sure whether everyone reading this knows what we are talking about.

G. Many will, for there are already several books written about them.* But there are many who are hearing this explanation for the first time.

L. Okay! What is a chief feature?

G. A chief feature is a characteristic that each of you has. When you are in the positive pole of this characteristic or feature, it can help you achieve your goals. When you are trapped in the negative pole, however, it keeps you from achieving your goals.

L. What do you mean by characteristic? Is it a characteristic that is unique to each one of us? Or is it a characteristic of the feature itself?

G. Good question! By characteristic, I mean the quality inherent in the chief feature itself. When you take on a particular chief feature, however, you take on its characteristics so that you appear to have the quality yourself. But you are really responding to the chief feature's quality.

L. I'm getting a bit confused. What is the purpose of the chief feature?

---

*See, for example, works by G. Gurdjieff such as *Life Is Real Only Then, When 'I Am'* (London: Arkana, n.d.), as well as Chelsea Quinn Yarbro, *Michael's People* (New York: Berkley Books, 1988); and Jose Sevens and Simon Warwick-Smith, *The Michael Handbook* (San Francisco: Warwick Press, 1990).

G. The purpose of the chief feature is a strange way to put it. The chief feature is not a part of your body system. You were not created with a flaw. You were created in the image and likeness of God! In no way have I put any sort of defect meant to cause you hidden challenges and conflict or problems. Let me say it again, YOU HAVE BEEN CREATED IN THE IMAGE AND LIKENESS OF GOD, OF LOVE!

L. Are we getting into some sort of religious question? I don't think the scope of this book can cover all the different religions in the world and all that they profess?

G. Perhaps it is a religious question to some. But I do not mean it as a religious question. For it is not a question of religion but of what you as a people have developed from generations and generations of not following your inner guidance.

L. What do you mean?

G. As you misused, over and over again, the inner tools that you have for living peacefully in your bodies, you developed fear to such a level that you don't even know that you are coming from fear. It has become what you think of as a natural part of you. You actually think that is how your system works best.

L. How did we get so far away from living in our bodies the way we were meant to?

G. You don't have to be so hard on yourself. You came into your body to learn more about yourself. To learn more about the love that you are. In the physical body you have experiences that you cannot have in spirit alone. In spirit, there is no fear. You are simply in your essence, which is love. In the physical body, you have the opportunity to learn about the love that you are, at another level. Understanding that all is love when you are feeling love is one thing. *Imagine feeling and knowing love when you are in fear. Imagine knowing that no matter what the situation on the outside, you are love and you can feel the strength and eternal quality of the love that you are.*

Let's get back to you and how you were feeling last night. When you were talking to your friend last night you went into your chief feature.

L. I did? How?

G. He was telling you about his day. You wanted to know more about how he was feeling. But even more important was how you were feeling. Instead of telling him about your vulnerability, you went into his vulnerability, distracting yourself from your own.

L. Go on. This is interesting. I hadn't looked at it that way before.

G. Yet that is what you were doing. You have opened yourself to another person, and so on a deep level your awareness is that what happens to him happens to you. Of course this is always true. What happens to one happens to all. But it is through your relationships that you feel it at a conscious level. At this level you can't deny the oneness of all creation. Relationship teaches you about oneness.

L. So if he is troubled, I am troubled.

G. Right.

L. How did my chief feature get involved?

G. Your chief feature is impatience—the fear of not having enough time, or of missing out. It puts you in a state of fear when you rush things. He was telling you of his experience in his own time and in his own way. When you are patient and coming from love, your questions "feel" different to him. His response is different. He responds openly and easily to the love you are coming from. But when you go into fear, he goes into fear, and you notice the shift. You put the blame on him, when in actuality, it was your fear. The place to look is inside of you.

L. I can see that now. I think we need to talk more about the chief features. They are so subtle and tricky.

G. Yes, indeed they are! **There are seven chief features:**

1. **Arrogance**
2. **Self-deprecation**
3. **Martyrdom**
4. **Impatience**
5. **Self-destruction**
6. **Greed**
7. **Stubbornness**

L. Would you explain each one?

G. Yes, but I want you to understand that the chief features are creations of your own. You, in your essential state, are love. Creating this twist to your life is your own doing. It is a clever twist, I'll give you that!

L. You sound so ungodlike when you act as if you aren't in control of everything.

G. And you think God is in control of everything? Wouldn't be much to free will if that were true!

L. Okay, okay. Maybe we can get into that at another time. I am still mystified by you.

G. And well you should be. I am quite the mystical character, wouldn't you say?

L. Oh yes, that you are. People have been talking about you as far back as recorded time. You have created a bit of a stir!

G. Thank you, my dear! On to the chief features! Although this is one thing you could be answering since it is one of your inventions.

L. Mine? I didn't create them!

G. No! I didn't mean "you" personally. I meant "you" collectively!

L. Oh! Even so, it is the part about fear and love that you can best help us with.

G. I would be glad to. Now, what was your question? Oh, yes, what are they? Well, sit back, take a deep breath, relax, and listen. This could take awhile. You'll find it revealing. See whether you can see yourself in any of them. But first I'll say a little more about you.

You are energy! Moving, flowing, feeling, fluid. Growth takes place when energy is flowing freely. Healing takes place when energy that is blocked is freed and flowing freely once again. Life is free flowing energy.

Love frees the flow of energy. Fear blocks the flow of energy. You are always choosing between love and fear. Both are powerful. When you are in fear, it seems there is no love. When you are in love, there is no fear. Choose one. Love or fear? Is your energy flowing freely, or is it blocked or scattered? The power is in the choosing.

You are in your earthly body to learn about love. Ironic, isn't it? Most of you are at war with your bodies. Love seems to have lost the battle. But has it? Can you feel yourself opening up to another way of living in your body? Knowing that what you have been doing no longer feels right, you are searching for more information and a deeper understanding of how your body works, of what your body needs.

Fear is the ultimate stumbling block!

Fear blocks you from being all that you are. It alone can keep you from making a phone call, raising your hand to answer or ask a question in a class or seminar, from making a free throw in basketball, giving a speech, asking someone for a date, making a commitment in a relationship, losing weight, attempting something new, writing a book, asking for a raise, having a child, healing, and even from expressing love.

Fear can also get you to make hasty decisions, to run away, to lash out at your best friend, to give up on living. You respond to fear as if fear were something to be afraid of. Fear confuses you, clouds your thinking, blocks your creative flow, and stops you cold in your tracks. Fear is a tricky devil! It disguises itself as mistrust, anger, greed, judgment, and impatience. It can be so difficult to see its true nature that you don't even know that you are in fear. Unaware that fear has overtaken you, you try, in vain, to resolve whatever details have arisen, instead of first, dissolving the fear.

When your physical, mental, emotional, and spiritual bodies are not nourished with what they need, your energy becomes blocked or scattered. Earlier in this book we discussed the needs of each of the bodies. Of all these needs, love is the greatest of all. Take care of love, and everything else will fall into place. Love is the key. Love is the answer. Love is the secret to health, happiness, and healing. Well! That's easy enough, wouldn't you say?

L. I know it sounds easy, but if it's so easy, why are there so many people who are not healthy, not happy, and not healing?

G. Alas! You decided that you needed a challenge. Something to make the game of life more interesting. Something that would enable you to delve deeper into the meaning of love. So you choose an obstacle or challenge that neutralizes movement towards your goal. And, of course, you all have a goal, a mission, a reason for being here. A goal that leads you to your ultimate reason for being in this earthly body—love!

L. This is where the chief feature comes in.

G. That's right.

L. Okay, so what exactly are the chief features?

G. I was just getting to that.

L. Good!

G. **The chief features:**

1. Arrogance is the fear of being judged.

There are many degrees or levels that you can slip into. Sometimes, it is mild, other times not so mild. People deeply trapped in the negative pole of arrogance will do anything they can to keep from being judged inadequate. Whether or not anyone is actually judging them is immaterial. In the negative pole, they feel as if everyone is judging them, as if they are in the spotlight. Actually, they are judging themselves. It can be quite brutal. Perfectionism runs rampant. They can't allow themselves to make any mistakes. Anything out of place or less than perfect bothers them.

Arrogance affects people differently, depending on their particular personality traits. It may surface only in certain areas of their lives. Often, they will go from one extreme of doing something very well to the other extreme of doing something very badly. Or they may not be willing to admit they have made a mistake or that they don't know something. They may not be open to new information because of the fear of appearing not to know something. They constantly judge themselves, appearing to be going along fine, when suddenly the smallest thing (the straw that breaks the camel's back) will upset them. They may not ask for help when they need it. If they become ill, they may hesitate in getting the help they need. In sport, they give their opponents too much credit and themselves too little; or they give opponents too little credit and themselves too much!

When they are in the negative pole (fear, of course), they are disrespectful of themselves or others. They may be loud and offensive. They can be haughty. They take on an "I'm worthy, you're not" attitude. Or "I'm okay, you're not," or "You're okay, I'm not" attitude.

Their thinking is no longer clear. They can be so angry that they can't see straight. They are not pleasant to be around when they are trapped in the negative pole. They are thwarted in movement toward their goals if they allow themselves to stay in the fear.

Many of you have chosen goals and lifestyles that take a lot of courage and confidence. You are out in front of people more than the average person. You have chosen leadership roles. This could be on a global scale or in regard to a much smaller scale. To fulfill your goal, you must know your strengths. You must have a proper perspective of what you can do.

When you are coming from the positive pole of this feature, you are confident, respectful of yourself and others, strong in moving toward your goals. You will feel especially good when you are coming from this place of strength and mutual respect. People will look to you for leadership.

Positive Pole:
Appropriate pride in self
Confidence
"I can do it attitude"
Leadership qualities
Ability to admit mistakes, learn from them, and move on
Respect for self and others

Negative pole:
Lack of respect for self and/or others
Low self-esteem, hidden under the show of superiority
Attachment to mistakes
Vanity
Perfectionism

2. Self-deprecation is the fear of being inadequate, not good enough, or of not being worthy.

People trapped in the negative pole of self-deprecation feel that they are not good enough. When faced with something new, they express doubt in their abilities. They may feel deep down that they are not worthy, that they do not deserve success, joy, or good relationships, that they are phonies, that they don't know what they are doing. When they get close to having what they want, they find reasons that they can't go for it, that they can't do it, that someone couldn't love them. They hesitate, fearful of being found inadequate. They apologize a lot. Sometimes they appear to be apologizing just for being. They need constant affirmation that they are worthy—affirmation from an outside source rather than from within. They often take on many tasks—so many that they can't do justice to them all—which leaves them feeling inadequate and frustrated.

In healing, they need to feel that they deserve healing, that they are worthy, even with whatever illness they may face. They may feel that they are letting others down, that whatever they do, it's not enough, and that they are not worthy of unconditional love.

In the negative pole, humility turns to self-defeating attitudes of unworthiness and just not being able to do everything. Many feel overwhelmed because they have a difficult time saying no. They can be heard saying, "I can't do it" or "I'm not good enough." Variations of those kinds of sentiments abound when they are in the negative pole. Of course, at the heart of it is the fear that they can't do it. That they truly are not worthy. They understand the magnificence of life and of God, but they compare and fear that they don't belong in the same playing field. But they do. It is only the fear talking.

People in the positive pole of self-deprecation are humble. They respect themselves and others equally. They know their abilities and use them to the highest degree. They go about their business quietly, achieving whatever they set out to do. There is not a lot of fanfare around them. They are often heard giving credit to others without putting themselves down.

This feature is particularly pleasant in the positive pole. Those of you who have chosen this quality demonstrate humility in its highest form. You are confident. You know that you can do anything, that you are good and you are worthy. Of course, you are. You are always helping others to see the good in them.

Positive Pole:
Humble
Respectful of self and others equally
Quiet confidence

Negative Pole:
Low self-esteem
Doubts self
Puts self down

.

146

3. Martyrdom is the fear of being the victim, of being trapped by circumstances or another person.

People trapped in the negative pole feel as if things never go well for them for very long. They have the "poor me" complex. They think that everyone and everything is against them. They often feel humiliated and embarrassed. They fear being the victim, and in this fear, they make themselves the victim. Nobody is doing it to them. They are doing it to themselves. Challenges happen to everyone, but people caught in martyrdom, feel it is worse for them. No one has it as bad as they do. They spend so much time focusing on how bad they have it that they don't have the energy to focus on the good in their lives. They are deeply attached to their wounds. They remember every grievance in their lives. Unless they can learn to detach from their wounds, to forgive and forget, they have a hard time healing.

They start expecting to be mistreated or unappreciated. The more they focus on what is happening to them, the deeper they go into fear, which will only get worse. When they don't get the proper appreciation for all that they have done, they feel like victims, that no one cares about them.

In the positive pole, they will go out of their way for others. They are always the first one to offer help to someone in need. They put other people's needs ahead of their own. Martyrs in history gave their lives for the greater good. They are the ones who are there in a crisis.

Positive Pole:
Helping others
Generous

Negative Pole:
Feeling of being the victim
Everything and everyone is against me
"Poor me"

4. **Impatience is the fear of not having enough time or of missing out.**

People in the negative pole of impatience can be scattered. They get ahead of themselves in their thinking, do not allow time for manifestation of their thoughts. They become frustrated that they are not doing enough, that they don't have enough time to do what they want to do. They jump ahead of themselves, skipping important steps along the way. They may be intolerant of people who seem to be taking too much time. In a discussion, if someone doesn't understand what he or she is saying, they may feel frustrated and just give up instead of slowing down and explaining their point of view with more information. When learning something new or training in sport, if they don't get it right away, they may give up out of frustration, feeling they just can't get it. What they really need is more training or practice. They get impatient when things don't happen quickly enough. They feel like they are running out of time. Whether they are or not has nothing to do with it. That is just how they feel. An anxiety comes over them when they are in the negative trap of impatience. They are often so patient in all other areas that it is hard to see themselves as impatient, or to see how impatience slows them down. They try to force things to go faster. This "forcing," of course, blocks the process.

In the positive pole, people become bold and daring. They see the quickest and most efficient way, are often able to bypass red tape. People often wonder how they get so much done in such a short time. They can also be the most patient people in the world because they understand the importance of patience. They see the path to their goals clearly and are able to keep their energy moving in the direction of their goals without being sidetracked. They are great to follow because they can usually find the best route. If you give them instructions, they know which ones you can combine or leave off entirely to get the job done quicker.

They are efficient because they can't stand to waste time doing things that don't need to be done. If you want to learn something as quickly as possible, a person in this pole will be a good teacher for you. He or she will know how to teach you in the quickest way possible. She cuts to the core of the process and throws out what isn't necessary. She explains things in simple terms.

Let's review the characteristics of each pole.

Positive Pole:
Patient
Efficient
Bold
In the moment

Negative Pole:
Frustrated
Anxious
Scattered
Intolerant

5. Self-destruction is the fear that life itself is not worth living.

In the extreme, self-destruction in the negative pole can be suicide. In lesser degrees, it sabotages success, relationships, happiness. People in self-destruction are just about to achieve their goals when they do something totally reckless. They fear losing control and so do things to prove that they are in control of everything. They dare anything or anyone to get in their way. They fear that life itself is not worth it—so why bother? The people in self-destruction seem to be their own worst enemies. In the negative pole, they get near accomplishing their goals, then self-destruct. They take unnecessary risks. They may take suicidal risks, careless risks. They may just want to end it all because they have no hope. They don't know the purpose of life. "What is it all for?" they may ask. They are in fear. They may try to control everything in the hope of finding some reason for life itself.

In the positive pole, these people would sacrifice their own lives for others. To a lesser degree, they sacrifice their desires for the good of others. They give you the shirt off their backs. They are quite often heroes, though they often die in the pursuit. They would run into a burning building to save a trapped child. They would literally give their lives to save others.

Positive Pole:
Sacrifice for the higher good

Negative Pole:
Suicide
Need to control everything
Self-sabotage

6. Greed is the fear of not having enough.

Persons caught in the negative pole of greed always want more. Whatever they have is not enough. Greed can manifest in many ways. In sport, these people must have any new piece of equipment that comes on the market. Or they never have enough training, enough points, enough matches, enough praise or attention. The sense of urgency about them feels like nervous energy. If it goes to food, they overeat, if to drink, they overdrink. If they are into personal growth, they can't read enough or go to enough seminars. They always need to know more. In the extreme, "having," no matter what it is, becomes an obsession. To heal, these people try everything. Afraid that they haven't tried it all, they want every pill, every form of healing available. They skip from one thing to the next without really giving anything a chance to make a difference.

This usually goes to basic survival stuff. They hoard things for fear that "someday" they may need them and be without them. They feel that their lives are at stake if they don't get whatever they feel they must have. In the negative pole they turn on you if they think you threaten their survival. They can be quite frantic about it.

In the positive pole, these people have a healthy appetite for what is available in life. The feature allows abundance, prosperity, health, joy, and love to flourish. People in the positive pole express passion for life. They go after the good things in life with zest! They explore deeply all their options. They have a thirst for living that is exciting. They want to see everything, do everything, meet everybody, and learn everything. They want life and all it has to offer.

Positive Pole

Healthy appetite
Zest for learning
Prosperity consciousness
Living life to the fullest

Negative Pole

Obsession with having more
Scarcity consciousness
Never satisfied that you have enough or have done enough
or know enough

7. Stubbornness is the fear of change.

People trapped in the negative pole of stubbornness are stuck. They are stuck in the way they are doing something, or in their thinking, or maybe in the way they see their world and themselves. You hear these people say, "I've always done it this way" or "This is just the way I am." They are closed to new information and different ways of doing things. This cuts them off from their inherent creativity because, of course, creativity is the source of change. Or they may be open to change and growth, but they inhibit the natural flow by putting limits on how and from whom they accept new information. They may dig their heels in and do something over and over again the same way, even though it isn't working. Athletes repeat the same strategy over and over again even though it is obvious to everyone watching that it doesn't work—as if they are shaking their head "no" to the change frequency of information coming into their energy fields.

They get stuck in "no." They have turned off the "yes" frequency. Creativity is almost nonexistent in the negative pole. They forget how resourceful they can be. They are scared to move out of their comfort zones. They have truly lost their way. They no longer know what they can do. They feel that they can only do it one way. And of course that way is not working. If things aren't going their way, they become defensive or withdraw their energies altogether.

But in the positive pole this stubbornness turns into determination. They work hours on end to finish something they started. They say they are going to do something, and by golly they do it no matter what! They stay with an idea, a process, or a skill until they have it. They are loyal. They are determined. When they go after something, they don't stop until they get it.

Positive Pole:
Determined
Steadfast
Firm
Loyal

Negative Pole:
Stuck
Closed to new information
Obstinate

So, there you have it! A description of each of the chief features. People tend to have one chief feature that traps them more than any other. But you can and do get caught in any number of them. Does that help you to understand these traps?

L.   Yes, very much. Thank you!

Highlights

1. Confusion is one way we stay stuck.

2. A chief feature is a characteristic that feels like a natural part of you.

3. Being trapped in the negative pole of your chief feature can block you from your goal.

4. There are seven chief features:

   • Arrogance

   • Self-deprecation

   • Impatience

   • Martyrdom

   • Greed

   • Self-destruction

   • Stubbornness

5. In the negative pole, fear is the basis of the chief feature.

6. Take care of the fear first.

14

Love Disguised as Fear

L. I heard a speaker last night talk about his experiences with angels. He also says that he was the apostle Paul.

G. And do you believe him?

L. I thought he was sincere. Whether or not he was apostle Paul, I don't really care. That is his concern, not mine.

G. What is your concern? Why did you go hear him speak?

L. I wanted to hear what he had to say. And I wanted to support him. His message is of love, I believe. And the more people spreading that message, the better.

G. What were your concerns about him?

L. That it was another man speaking. That when he spoke of the life of Jesus and the Bible, it was all about men.

G. It is a trap men have fallen into. Believing that it is all about male energy. Fearing that if they don't hold onto their "power," they lose. The fear is that there is not enough. That they will lose out on something if they don't stay in power, if they don't keep women in "their place." It is still a strong fear in your world.

L. Is there anything I can do to help? To help dissolve this fear of there not being "enough" for everyone? I want people to understand that no one needs to have power over another. We all can be empowered.

G. That is very good. Self-empowerment is love. Power over anyone is based in fear. It will always be a source of pain for you in the body. As long as someone feels the need to have power over another, they will not be at peace. For, of course, "power over" needs constant "outside" vigilance. As I have said, to live in peace in your body, you must have the vigilance "inside" you. Awareness! Awareness of your thoughts, ideas, emotions, attitudes, the care of your body—all of your body. Living each and every moment from who you truly are. Being you in each and every moment. Knowing that what you do is important. It is important in the creation of you. What you do, think, say, and express is creating your story. That is where your power is. From within you. That is always there. Yours. It can never be taken from you. You can turn it over to someone or something else. But you do it by your choice. You choose that by the choices you make in any and every moment of your life.

L. Choose wisely?

G. Choose with awareness! Know what you choose. Know that you are always making choices. Choices to come from fear or to come from love.

L. Ah! We are back to the question of why anyone would choose to come from fear? You mentioned a desire to know the other side. Of what other side were you speaking?

G. The other side of love! Fear is the other side of love. You wanted to know what love felt like when you were in fear.

It is why you have chosen to be in a body.

L. To know fear? That wasn't too smart!

G. No! To know love. To go deeper into love. To know your-self at deeper and deeper levels. To experience love. To experience more of yourself. It is grand, isn't it? When you feel love at these deeper and deeper levels it often brings you to tears, does it not?

L. Yes! I have noticed that when I am working with clients they may start crying. They say they don't know why be-cause they are not sad.

G. They are feeling love. They have been so out of love, that when they tune into love again, it is an incredible feeling. They want more of it. Have you noticed the lightness about people after this experience?

L. Yes! It is one of the great joys I have in doing my work.

G. They are having essence contact.

L. Essence contact?

G. Yes! They are connecting with their souls. With the love that they are. With their essence, with their core! It's won-derful! Beautiful! The more you live from your essence, the more of your true self you express, the more you live in love.

L. How does this explain why we want to learn about fear? The other side of love, as you say?

G. Learn about fear! Yes! That is why. Not because you want to come from fear. But because you want to learn more about love.

L. Wait a minute! I thought we were talking about fear?

G. We are! As I said earlier, fear is love disguised.

L. I think I am getting it.

G. Exactly!

Love Disguised as Fear

Learn to dissolve the fear and uncover the love.

You are made in the image and likeness of God. God is love! I am love. So all that exists comes originally from love. But somewhere along the line, you lost your way. And love seems to have disappeared. But of course it hasn't. It is still there. The love is there. Uncovering the love, allowing the love to express itself, is what life in a body is all about!

L. So learning about fear is one way to uncover love?

G. Yes! Fear is your creation, not mine. Believe me when I tell you that fear keeps you from experiencing all that you are. And fear gives you the opportunity to experience all that you are. It gives you the opportunity to choose, to consciously choose love. To be consciously aware of the love that you are. Without fear, there was no need for awareness. You just were. You just were love.

Have you noticed that when you thought you lost something and then you found it, how much more you appreciated it? Your understanding of it was deeper for having momentarily lost it. It is a phenomena that can be experienced in the body system, not one that can be experienced in spirit form.

L. This is getting more and more complicated.

G. Perhaps you would prefer to leave out some of the "why" things are the way they are and just stick to how things are —what you have the power to create and how to access this power?

L. The "why" is intriguing. But I don't see how we can answer those questions now. It doesn't seem like there ever could be a definitive answer to these questions.

G. The answers to these questions are within each of you.
    You have to answer these questions yourself. No one can
    give you the answer to your own "why." That is why "you"
    can't answer the "why" question for anyone else.

L. That makes sense to me. I am always questioning other
    people when they tell me answers that may be right for
    them but not for me.

G. Of course you are! You are each experiencing life in a body
    from your own perspective. Discovering who you are is a
    very personal experience. And a collective one.

L. A collective one?

G. Yes! Each one of you has a piece of the puzzle that makes
    up the whole. When one of you opens up and becomes
    more conscious, more aware, more of the love that you
    are, it creates a space for everyone else to open and be-
    come more aware. To become more of the love they are.

L. So that's why it's important to see the oneness.

G. Yes, each of you has an answer. No one person has all the
    answers. You need each of you to be all that you are, all
    the love that you are, for the picture to be complete. And
    your body is part of this creation. You are using your body
    to experience this life, this way of knowing more of who
    you are. Thus it is vital that you live in peace and harmony
    with your body. Your body is your way, the vehicle that
    will get you to where you are going. Which, of course, is
    simply back to yourself. Together you have all the answers
    you seek. Alone you only have your piece of the puzzle.
    Still, you are quite complete alone. But not totally.

Never are you all of you without all of you!

Highlights

1. Self-empowerment is love.

2. "Power over" is based in fear.

3. As long as you feel you need to have "power over" someone, you will not be at peace in your body.

4. Your choices are to act from fear or from love.

5. Choose with awareness.

6. Fear stops you from expressing all that you are, and fear gives you the opportunity to express all that you are.

7. Fear gives you the opportunity to choose love .

8. If you can see love in fear, you can learn to dissolve the fear and uncover the love.

9. Only you can answer the "why" of your life.

10. Peace and harmony are vital to the body.

11. Each of you has a piece of the puzzle that makes up the whole.

12. Never are you all of you without all of you.

15

The Freedom
of Appreciation

L. I feel great! It is a beautiful day here in Minnesota! One of those fall days when the warmth of the sun is appreciated like no other time of the year. Soon the winter winds will be blowing through the land. The sun feels particularly good this time of the year.

G. Do you know why the sun feels "particularly" good this time of the year?

L. Well, sure. Because we know that winter is coming. That before we know it, it will be cold. The warmth of the sun will be gone until spring. We want to savor every ray!

G. That's right! You have added appreciation to the mix. Appreciation always adds sweetness to whatever you are doing or to whomever you are with. It's a key ingredient in your life. One that I am afraid is not used as often as it needs to be in order to be effective.

L. What do you mean? A key ingredient?

G. Just that. In your story, your creation, your life, you need appreciation in heavy doses. Appreciation is one of the inner tools you have to make your life the way you desire.

The Freedom of Appreciation

L. How does appreciation actually work? What is its purpose?
G. First, think of appreciation as one of your inner tools.

Appreciation is something that you appear to give to someone else or even for something. Your appreciation for the beautiful day appears to be for something. And it is. But how appreciation works is quite interesting. It is always a win-win proposition for whomever or whatever is involved in the appreciation. Yet appreciation is a tool for your benefit. It benefits the person who is using it. All of your inner tools work this way. But because of their dual nature, the benefit to yourself is often misunderstood. Appreciation is a tool that can be used for several reasons.

L. What are they? I thought appreciation was just a way of saying thank you.
G. And it is! But that is only one side of it. Appreciation is meant to:

1. **Bring you back into the moment**
2. **Get your blocked energy moving**
3. **Lighten your energy**
4. **Help your body go to higher performance levels.**
5. **Help you to stay on your path or move back on your path**
6. **Motivate you to do something you want to do**
7. **Inspire you**
8. **Increase your understanding of someone or something**
9. **Make you feel better**

L. Wow! Appreciation does all that?
G. Yes! That is the purpose of the tool of appreciation.

L. I can see all of it. But . . .

G. But? But what?

L. But isn't it phony to "use" appreciation to "get" something?

G. Yes! If your appreciation isn't sincere, it won't work. After all, then it wouldn't really be appreciation. You would be using deception perhaps. In fact, it would backfire. And you would feel worse instead of better. You must use your tools correctly for them to be effective. Many of you use them incorrectly and then wonder why they don't work.

L. If we are meant to be able to pull out appreciation from our "bag of tricks" when we need it for the reasons you stated, how can that be sincere? Aren't we, by the very nature of choosing it for those reasons, being insincere?

G. Oh, Linda! You do have some distorted ideas! Let's say that you received a gift in the mail. Do you not choose to write a thank-you note?

L. Yes, of course! But that isn't for me. That is because I am genuinely grateful for the gift.

G. How do you "feel" when you receive a gift and you don't write or call to say thank you?

L. How do I "feel?" Well, let's see . . . I feel like my energy is not flowing freely. There is a sense of something that needs to be done.

G. Now, let's say you write or call to say thank you. You express appreciation. How do you feel?

L. Like my energy is free again. I feel lighter. I feel good.

G. Didn't you choose to write or say thank you?

L. Yes, but my intention wasn't to make me feel better. It was to make the person who sent the gift feel good.

The Freedom of Appreciation

G. Here is where you are not being totally honest with yourself. A part of you is choosing to show appreciation so that YOU will feel better. You did the right thing! You have gotten so far off track, as far as some of these inner tools are concerned, that you don't even know that they truly are meant to help you.

L. Keep going—this is getting interesting. I'm starting to see what you mean.

G. Everything in your body is for you. It is all about you.

L. Isn't that a bit selfish? I think I do quite a few things for other people.

G. At the core of everything you do, you will find "you." Of course you will. This is your life—your body, mind, heart, and spirit. This is your soul's journey. If giving to someone else is a part of your soul's journey, is it not for you that you give? The giving helps you, serves you. Perhaps what you give benefits someone else. But the giving itself is for you. You alone! You are the recipient of the gift of giving.

L. All right, but how can we show appreciation sincerely, if we know we are doing it for ourselves? It still feels phony if we are doing it for ourselves.

G. Linda, you really have to get past this idea that you have about doing things for others. Everything you do is for your benefit. This is your life. You are creating the very fiber of your story with the tools you choose to use. If appreciation is a tool you use every day, often during the day, in every moment of your life, your life will take on the lightness, the joy, the love that is expressed in appreciation. You become what you express.

Your energy flows the way it does as a direct result of the inner tools you use in each and every moment of your life, regardless of the situation or circumstances.

Can you understand that? Yes, of course others are affected by what you do. You are all one. How could all not be affected? That doesn't mean what you do is not done for you. All that you do, think, and express makes up who you are. That is how you are creating YOU! Or more accurately, that is how you are recreating you!

L. So how do we use appreciation the way it is meant to be used? As a tool?

G. Okay. Let's use an example of something going on in someone's life in which the tool of appreciation might be used. Or that you might advise them to use. Let's pretend John is your client. John is an athlete. Golf is his sport. He is having trouble with his game. He can't seem to stay focused on golf. His mind wanders all over the place. He finds himself getting angry and frustrated when he doesn't play as well as he thinks he can. When he calls you, he complains about all the things going wrong in his life. He gets more upset the longer he complains.

L. This sounds familiar. Have you been bugging my phone?

G. What do you think? Let's get back to John. The first thing you notice is how out of the moment he is. No wonder he can't stay focused. He is angry about what he doesn't have. Appreciation brings you back into the moment. So it could be one tool to help him. He, in fact, isn't feeling very appreciated himself. What did I say appreciation does for you?

L. A number of things. It brings you back into the moment. Unblocks your energy. Motivates and inspires you. Enhances your body's level of performance by freeing your energy. Helps you to understand what is going on.

G. Wouldn't you say our friend John could use all of that?

L. Yes, he sure could.

G. Okay! So we tell John to focus on what he likes about his life. About his game. About the environment around him. We shift him from complaining and worrying to appreciating and feeling better. Once he starts appreciating what he has, he feels a shift in his energy. It starts to flow again. He is more patient and understanding with himself. His body is free of the criticism he was heaping upon it, and thus he moves more smoothly. His swing is uninhibited. He is relaxed when he putts. There are no glitches in his movements. He feels the silence as he putts for birdie.

L. Did we miss a step? Honestly, I'm not sure how we got John to express appreciation.

G. Honestly is the only way appreciation can be expressed. If it isn't honest, it's not appreciation, is it?

L. No, it isn't. Still, when we don't feel happy about what is going on in our lives, it's hard to express appreciation.

G. True. But it is no harder than expressing lack of appreciation. It is just the other side of the coin. So how do we get John to do it? First, we tell him to take a deep breath. Notice how deep breathing is a part of all the processes to call on your inner tools. Deep breathing helps you to relax just enough to gain access to your toolbox. Being frantic doesn't work. Then we have John place his attention on his heart area. He can gently rub his heart area if he needs help in

getting his attention there. As he breathes in, he listens. If
nothing pops up at that instant that he appreciates in his
life, then we tell him to visualize or remember someone or
something in his life that he likes. He need not think, just
feel! When something comes up, bless that person, using
the image of light. Bathe that person in light, allowing the
love within to be expressed towards the person. No thoughts
are necessary, just love. Feel the love.

L. How is it supposed to feel?

G. Good grief, woman! Everyone knows what love feels like.
He may need just a few moments for love to express itself
naturally. Of course, appreciation is a form of love. It feels
like love in your body. Love is energy flowing freely. In
your heart area, there is a particularly good feeling. If you
have suppressed love in your life, it will take awhile for it
to be felt. It is there. Keep breathing and bathing yourself,
as well, in love, while imagining this person or thing. John
will notice that he is starting to calm down. He is beginning to feel better. Whenever he starts to come out of appreciation, he goes back into his frustration. But it is a
little less intense this time. Gently guide him back into
appreciation. Out of his head and back into his heart. He
needs to do this consistently. After awhile he will notice a
substantial difference in how he feels. How he feels when
he is "doing" appreciation will be different from how he
feels when he isn't. The idea is to do it so often that it
becomes a natural part of you. You become appreciation.
There is no separation between doing and not doing appreciation. It feels so good, you do it all the time. The more
he practices it off the course, as well as on the course, the
better he will be at it, and the faster he will be able to change

his state. It is a tool. You must learn how to use these tools correctly, and you must practice to become competent with them.

L. I don't think people realize that these tools can be used to achieve the results we desire. They are not the result or accomplishment or the thing desired. They are the tools to achieve those things. And you need to practice using the tools to learn how to use them effectively.

Okay, back to John. When he starts to use appreciation it moves him back into the moment. It is easy for him to focus on his golf when he is playing because that is what he is doing and he is in the moment.

G. Exactly. He has no thoughts of anything else. He is in sync. Body, mind, heart, and spirit are all in tune. He almost immediately notices an improvement in how his body performs. He appreciates his body. His body, in turn, gives him what he desires. He feels better.

L. All in the name of appreciation!

G Yes!

L. So his whole day becomes one of appreciation.

I have another story of a tennis athlete who used appreciation to change her state and her energy. Because she has been training with her inner tools she was able to do it more quickly than John could. Susan was playing a team match. Her first match of the day was a doubles match. She had been up almost the whole night with one of the other team members who was sick and going through a tough time. When she got to the courts in the morning, she wasn't in a very good mood. She was tired and wondered whether she was in any shape to play both her doubles and singles matches. Yet she knew the team needed her. She couldn't quite get it together for her doubles match. She was scattered and easily moved into negative thinking. Her attention was divided between the events of the night before and her singles match yet to be played. With her attention in the past and future, it was no wonder her shots lacked their usual precision and authority. She was furious with herself after they lost the doubles match, a match she felt they should have won! I talked to her after the match. I told her that we needed her to play her singles match from strength. That she needed to let go of the doubles match and her anger. That she needed to change her state and get ready for her next match. And she had only ten minutes to do it!

Bless her heart. In ten minutes she was a new person, ready and eager to play her singles match. What a difference it made. She went out and played one of the best matches of the year. The poor girl she played didn't have a chance! Susan won 6–0, 6–0!

G. That's quite a story! Tell us how she did it. How did she change her state so quickly?

L. That's the best part. It is exactly what we have been discussing. She told me that she started thinking about all the other things she could be doing that weren't nearly as exciting or appealing as playing tennis. She also thought about other people and how much worse off they were than she is. People starving to death, people at war with each other, people losing their homes, people having to pay for their education while she was able to earn it by playing tennis. She thought, "I have it pretty good. What am I getting so upset over? This is only a tennis match! And besides, I love tennis!"

G. That's beautiful! You can easily see with that example how appreciation is a tool that can bring you back into the present moment and get your energy flowing smoothly. I'm sure her opponent didn't know what hit her. That kind of energy is powerful. Her intention was clear. All of her attention was on the playing of each and every point, one at a time.

Where your attention goes, so goes your energy!

L. I love that story! Until you practice using appreciation when you least feel it, you won't know its power to change your state. Sometimes when I use it, it feels as if I have cleaned up some garbage. I feel cleaner and lighter! It feels great. I am moving forward instead of backwards.

G. You have it! Appreciation is meant to be used often. The more often the better. Use it every day for just one month, and you will see an incredible difference in your life. You will feel a vibrancy about your energy that you didn't feel before. Your outlook on life itself will change. You will have to experience it to really know the power of this tool.

L. Thank you for that explanation. I know we have talked about appreciation before, but I never really looked at it from an energy perspective as I do now. I can feel how it changes my energy. My energy feels lighter and quicker somehow. I do feel the vibrancy you spoke of.

G. Tell us where in your body you are feeling something. Where are you feeling the lightness?

L. I'm glad you asked that question. Just before you did, I was noticing the energy in my heart area. It was increasing. The good feeling was getting stronger. I was even feeling a smile come across my face. Yes, it definitely is in my heart area.

G.   Yes, of course! Appreciation is heart energy. Enjoy it. It will last for a long time. As long as you stay in that frame of mind.

L.   What do you mean, frame of mind?

G.   Your thoughts. As long as you think thoughts that take you down the path of appreciation, you will benefit from the energy. You will be in the energy of lightness and love. You will feel the flow of your energy. You will feel alive with all that you have. With all that you are. Appreciate everything and everyone in your life. Every moment of your life.

When you find yourself feeling as if you don't have enough, that is when to use appreciation.

When you feel as if you can't do enough, that is when to use appreciation. When you feel as if there are not enough relationships in your life, that is when to use appreciation. Yes, appreciation is meant to be used for what you have. Not just when you receive something. That is only one moment. Surely having something for a period of time doesn't take away from its value, now does it?

L.   No, you are right, of course. It doesn't. Yet, it does seem to lose some of its value somehow.

G.   Either it does, or it doesn't. Which is it? Does the mere fact of having something or someone in your life for a period of time take away from its value? What do you think?

L.   No, of course it doesn't. But . . .

G. But what? But nothing. It doesn't lose its value. You have merely chosen to take it for granted. You have chosen not to use the tool of appreciation.

L. But you know there are things that maybe I no longer do appreciate. Maybe time has taken away its value.

G. No! It is not the time that has devalued it. Perhaps you have changed. Perhaps you no longer do feel the same about it.

L. Then what do we do? Do we try to appreciate it anyway?

G. No, of course not. Appreciation, like all your inner tools, is meant to be used honestly. If you don't truly appreciate something or someone, you can't fake it and expect the tool to change your energy. Remember, you can't fool yourself. You always know the truth. All your tools work beautifully but only with honesty. You cannot fake it.

L. So what do we do? If there are things in our lives that we no longer appreciate, do we just throw them away?

G. Yes! Or recycle them.

L. What about the people in our lives that we no longer appreciate?

G. Stay up to date with what you have and who is in your life. Check it out. Anything in your life that you don't appreciate should move on. Check out your things, your clothes, your objects, everything. If you no longer appreciate something, it's time for it to move on, too.

How many things do you have stored in your home that you no longer have any use for? Someone, somewhere needs it. Recycle! When you do this, you will notice a freeing of your energy, too. You will then have created a space for something new to come in.

L. That is fine for things, but we can't recycle people.

G. No, not recycle! People come and go in your lives. Some of them stay a lifetime. Some of them come for a particular time in your life, for a particular reason. Some are not meant to stay in your life for your whole life. Recognizing when it is time to move on is an important element to staying in the flow. To staying in the flow of life. Hanging on to someone who is meant to go on only causes your energy to be blocked. But this is a topic we can get into at another time. People and relationships are a whole book unto itself.

L. Yes, another book! I remember you said something about a book about relationships. So we are going to save this conversation for another time?

G. Yes! Now do you have any other questions about appreciation?

L. No. What you have told us is very helpful. Appreciation is a tool I will use often. I like the idea of using it every day for a month. How can I know its power if I don't use it?

G. Appreciation will also open you up to using other tools.

L. Such as confidence?

G. Yes. Now it is important to remember to gather your energy before you do something. When Susan took the time to use appreciation, she was also gathering her energy. Whenever you want to do something that requires more energy or requires you to express more of who you are, you must allow your energy to shift and build, then release it at the appropriate time. This is what Susan did so well in her prematch preparation. Then, when she began playing, she released her energy into her tennis.

L. Do you think people will understand what a powerful tool appreciation is? After all, I don't think it has been thought of as a tool before, much less a powerful one. It seems the opposite of force.

G. And well it is! Linda, it is not your job to make sure people use their tools correctly. That is up to each and every person to do on their own. You have no control over that. Your job is to teach what you know to be the truth. Each person reading this will accept or reject this teaching according to his or her own experience. You do your part. That is all you can do. Just as you can't control who wins a tennis match, you can't control how people receive this information. You do your part. That is all anyone can do.

L. That sounds good. There is a sense of peace in knowing that I only need to do my part.

G. Yes, and every time that you come from love, you will find your part is enough. You have been given everything you need, within you, to live the life you desire. To fulfill the mission you have taken on. To find yourself. To know love in all its forms.

L. Wow! It is so easy to forget why I am here in the first place. I get caught up in what is happening, instead of who I am and how I am manifesting the who that I am.

G. Yes.

The secret to living in a body is to remember that you are not your body.

Remember who you are. When you come from who you are and not what you are or where you are or the situation you are in, you cannot go wrong. You are love. When you forget that you find yourself lost and bewildered.

L. Why is that so hard to get? Like right now, I understand it, and I feel the truth of it. In a few moments, though, I could feel totally different. Caught up in an emotion that drags me down.

G. That is why you must use your inner tools. One of which is discipline.

You must learn to discipline your thoughts.

To guide them down the path you truly desire. You have free will. You can go anywhere with them that you wish. You will all end up in the same place. The destination is the same for everyone. Which road you take is up to you. Do not judge someone for taking a harder road. A road of sickness and hardship is not necessarily the wrong path. You don't know anyone else's soul journey. It's not up to you to decide anyone else's path. Each of you must do that for yourself. You cannot know someone else's path. Pain and misery for one may be another soul's way of knowing love at another level all together. You do not know.

L. Then are we to just allow sickness and misery? Shall we do nothing when we see what we perceive to be an injustice?

G. You are to do whatever you feel is right for you. If helping someone feels right for you, do it. Live your life according to your inner guidance. It is the only way home.

L. Home! Hmmm!

G. Do you doubt that you are on a journey home?

L. It just seems so far away, sometimes.

G. Only when you have moved out of your true essence is it far away. Stay in love, and you will always be at home. You asked for instructions to living in a body. I am giving you these instructions. If you choose not to follow them, that is your free will. You, and only you, can decide how you want to live your life. How to create your life. Do you want to live in love? Do you want to live in fear?

L. So you are saying that it doesn't matter what we choose—love or fear—because the destination is the same?

G. Yes. You are all rediscovering the love that you are. Whether you choose to go through fear to find love or you choose to go through love to find love is up to you.

L. Doesn't it make more sense to go through love? Why would anyone want to go through fear?

G. To discover love in all things. The choice is always yours. Life will happen. You will be given opportunities to choose love. Ultimately you will choose love. It is just a matter of which route you take. What do you want? It is your choice.

L. I want love, of course.

G. Do not say "of course" as if there is no other choice. That is where you get confused. There are many choices. You are always choosing. Choose wisely, and appreciate each step of your journey.

Highlights

1. Appreciation always adds sweetness to whatever you are doing or to whomever you are with.

2. Appreciation benefits the giver as well as the receiver.

3. Appreciation is one of your most powerful inner tools.

4. Appreciation:
   - Brings you back into the moment
   - Unblocks your energy
   - Lightens your energy
   - Helps your body to perform at high levels
   - Helps you stay or move back on your path
   - Motivates you
   - Inspires you
   - Increases your understanding
   - Makes you feel better

5. Appreciation is real only when it is sincere.

6. You become what you express.

7. Where your attention goes, so goes your energy.

16

The Body Speaks

L. It seems like such a long time since we last wrote together. I'm not sure where I would like to begin. You have been directing the flow. I'd like you to continue. You've done a pretty good job so far!

G. Thank you, Linda. What have you been experiencing over the last four days?

L. I've been sick. I have a cold!

G. You don't sound very pleased.

L. I'm not! I don't know why I got sick! I want to be healthy and strong.

G. And getting a cold isn't part of the plan?

L. No, it certainly isn't.

G. And why not?

L. What do you mean, why not? No one wants to be sick.

G. Perhaps not on a conscious level. But let's suppose that on another level, it is your body's way of speaking to you. Your body's way of letting you know that you are off balance or off the track (so to speak).

L. Couldn't it just let me know in an easier way than through a cold? Do I have to get sick?

G. Did you have to get sick? No, of course not. But how often do you listen to your body, giving it what it needs?

L. I think I do a pretty good job of listening to my body.

G. And giving it what it needs?

L. Yes.

G. Linda, Linda, Linda, this is ME you are talking to! Do you remember when we talked about honesty.

L. Yes! You said that being honest, totally honest with oneself, is vital to our well-being and to our achieving our potential.

G. So let's be honest. What are some of the messages your body has been giving you?

L. Oh, I don't think I'm going to like this process!

G. Of course you will. The truth will set you free! Truth and honesty always make you feel better. It is getting the truth out that sometimes causes discomfort. But that is only because you are allowing fear to block your energy.

L. Fear? How did fear get involved?

G. Oh, you can bet fear is involved any time you're not feeling well.

L. What messages has my body been sending me? Okay! I know it has been telling me that I need to start stretching every day.

G. And what good is stretching?

L. Well, my body would be more flexible. I could move easier. It wouldn't hurt so much after I have been sitting in certain positions for a long time.

G. What other messages have you been receiving?

L. That I need to get more rest.

G. Tell us how you feel?

L. I have a headache. My nose is running. I feel congested, and my energy is low. I have the sniffles, and I sneeze a lot.

G. A cold is telling you that your body needs something. It is telling you that your resistance is down, that you are not taking care of your body in the way it needs to be cared for. A "cold" is a good way to describe how your body feels. Out in the cold. Not being taken care of. It is getting cold treatment! What other messages have you received?

L. I was afraid we weren't done with that question!

G. Be not afraid, my child! I am here to help you. I'm on your side! This is not to blame you. This is not to reprimand you! This is to help you see the truth.

L. I know. So why am I afraid—hesitant at the very least?

G. Because the truth also carries responsibility. Once you consciously acknowledge that you have heard your body speak, ignoring it is difficult. That means you will have to make some sort of change.

L. And we're not crazy about change!

G. That's right! For some reason you have developed this fear of change.

All life is about change. It is the essence of life. Yet you can take much comfort from the knowledge that your essence and the essence of life never changes.

It is always about love. You are love. All is love.

L. I think you need to be a little more specific here. Are people just supposed to sit around doing nothing?

G. No, that's not it at all!

Awareness of the love that you are transforms your life from a life focused on acquiring to a life of living— living the you that you are.

You are to live from love rather than from fear. This makes all the difference. Love has many disguises. Love comes in the form of trust, belief, courage, confidence, discipline, fun, joy, light, laughter, smiles, knowing, patience, determination, happiness, feeling, being, doing, to name just a few.

L. Go on. I like this idea.

G. Okay. Pretend that you are an athlete. Golf is your sport. Your mission, should you accept it, is to demonstrate love through your golf game.

L. Keep going. This is getting good.

G. Thank you! So if your mission is to demonstrate love through your golf, how might you do that?

L. By playing with joy and enthusiasm. By playing with love.

G. Yes! But how does that manifest in a golf game? How do we see it in our golfer? Be specific.

L. For the golfer, it isn't really about the physical aspect of the game. It is about how the person responds to all the different things that come up during a round of golf.

G. For instance, what happens on the golf course for this golfer to demonstrate love?

L. Earlier we learned that the body needs clear messages from the mental body to the emotional body, which in turn fuels the physical body. The higher-level thoughts fuel higher-level emotions, which in turn raise the level of performance of the body. During a round of golf, the obstacles that show up give our golfer a chance to respond from any level. Just as in life. If you respond with higher-level thoughts, the body will respond in turn.

G. For instance?

L. For instance, our golfer just misses a birdie putt. This is a situation that happens frequently. Just missing the hole, or even rolling in, then out.

G. How does our golfer respond?

L. With love!

G. You'd better explain that one a bit more, or you are going to lose half your audience. They'll think you are Pollyanna!

L. And what's wrong with Pollyanna?

G. Now, Linda, you do know what I mean! Love is misunderstood today. That is why I said love has many disguises. You don't always recognize the power of love or how to trigger this power to achieve your desire. When you say that our golfer responds with love, many people really don't know what you mean. They have forgotten what love can do. They have forgotten what love is.

Love is your energy moving freely.

When your energy is moving freely, your body is at its best. It is in tune with your intuition. Your fine motor skills are uninhibited. Your entire body is moving without a glitch. And you feel great. Your thinking is clear. You are moving forward. You are not stuck.

You are always giving your body messages about what you want it to do for you. Your body is there for you. It wants to do whatever you ask of it. Your body is at your service. Take care of it, and it will more than take care of you. It loves to perform at the high levels it knows.

L. So what does our golfer do? What is the response that comes from love?

G. It is very much like what you told our tennis player, Martina. After the missed putt, you will need to direct your mental body. Remember, your mental body can go all over the place. It can just as easily criticize as encourage you. What do you think your body will best respond to? Criticism or encouragement?

L. Encouragement, of course.

G. That's right. That is how your body was created. It, like you, was made in the image and likeness of God! And who is God? Love! Whether you call me God, Goddess, Buddha, All that Is, The Source, The Universe, The I Am, whatever name you call me, I am love. You are love. All is love.

Come from love in all that you are, and you will be free to be all that you are.

L. So life is the expression of love. That's it, isn't it? It isn't about winning the golf game or making a lot of money, or even about the relationships we have? It is about expressing who we are in all that we do, in all that we are.

G. Bingo! You've got it, But let's stay specific. Back to our golfer. Our golfer is manifesting the self through golf.

L. Which means that if our golfer responds from a place of love, she will play better.

G. Exactly!

L. We'd better go over that a bit more. What exactly did our golfer do that was from love?

G. Good idea. Our golfer missed the birdie putt. Many responses are possible. If our golfer chooses to respond from fear instead, we see fear demonstrated through anger, disappointment, frustration, impatience, and maybe even disrespect. But this golfer knows that her mission is to demonstrate love through the playing of golf. So she responds with a quick bit of encouragement to the body. She lets her body know that it's okay, she is still with it. She still believes in it. She takes a deep breath, allowing her to relax and go to a place of peace. A slight correction, a bit of instruction—that is all she needs. Thus she is free to move on to the next hole without any residue from the last shot. In fact, the body has a positive experience to draw from, instead of a negative experience that would just drain its energy. How do you think she feels approaching the next hole?

L. Clear and in the moment. She will be enjoying the game. Totally in the present. She will be feeling pretty confident because she hasn't allowed anything to distract her. She has stayed in love energy.

G. Which means that her energy is flowing freely.

L. Exactly!

G. During a round of golf, any number of challenges arise. It is the nature of the game. It is life played out before your eyes. How do you respond to the challenges? How do you respond to life? Which tools do you choose to use? Higher-level tools or lower-level tools? This goes along with the analogy of your inner tools to the typewriter and the computer. The typewriter works, but the computer works much better. Anger may work, but encouragement works a lot better.

L. What about the fear people have that if you encourage a child too much he will become spoiled and lazy?

G. Encouragement does not lead to laziness. But if encouragement is the only tool that is taught, the child will not know how to use his body effectively and may become discouraged instead of encouraged. You must teach your children about all the inner tools they have. Children are begging you to teach them. They may say "Sports aren't fun," or "I don't like it. It isn't any fun!" They are begging you for help. They know that life is meant to be joyful. They know that something is wrong. They just don't know how to fix it. Now, you can tell them.

L. Me?

G. All of you. It does take a village to raise a child. Treasure them. Teach them well.

L. What are we supposed to tell them?

G. Tell them about the power of love. Teach them about love. Teach them how to come from love in all that they do.

L. Some people might find that boring or silly.

G. Boring or silly! Then you have not taught them love. You must teach them about tools such as curiosity, passion, responsibility, honesty, determination, courage, persistence, and desire. You must teach them how to discipline their mental bodies, or they will surely go crazy. Discipline is a powerful tool.

L. Discipline isn't appreciated much.

G. That is because you don't know what it is. Discipline is really guidance.

Without guidance, your body doesn't know which way it is going.

Since you have free will, you are free to go in any direction. Without discipline or guidance, you will go any which way, never really knowing where you are going. Remember, discipline is guidance. It is meant to be used with gentleness and firmness. When used properly, the guidance that it gives will be clear and pure. Your body will receive the information without any distortions. Your body will respond positively because the guidance makes sense. Your body will know that the discipline it is receiving is for its highest good. Your body is always reaching for its highest good. Always!

L.   How can people learn to discipline or guide their bodies with gentleness and firmness? That isn't how a lot of people use discipline. Discipline is almost a form of punishment.

G.   That is where you got off track. Discipline was never meant to be used as a punishment. It became a punishment because it was being used from a place of fear rather than love.

L.   How do you mean, from fear? I guess I was talking about someone disciplining someone else. Like a parent disciplining a child, for instance.

G.   What you are talking about isn't discipline, although that is the name you give it. That is yelling, screaming, hitting, pushing, blaming, or a number of other things. The parent doesn't know what to do and is afraid the child will continue doing something the parent considers wrong. The parent goes into fear—coming from a place of fear in how he or she is responding to the child.

L.   Boy, do I see that. With my children, Josh and Lisa, I would respond negatively when I was in fear. It didn't work very well at all. Now I know better!

Highlights

1. Illness is one way your body communicates with you that it needs something.

2. Total honesty with yourself is vital to your well-being and to achieving your goals.

3. The truth carries responsibility with it.

4. Change is a part of life.

5. The essence of life, however, is never changing. It is always love.

6. You are always giving your body messages— your body needs these messages to be clear.

7. Life is the expression of love.

8. Encouragement doesn't lead to laziness.

9. Teach your children the power of love.

10. Discipline from love is a form of guidance.

11. Discipline from fear is a form of punishment.

17

Opening the Heart

G. There is a shift happening in the energy in your universe. A shift to heart energy. You will notice it in every aspect of life. Men and women both are going to notice it. You need to learn more about your emotional body and how it functions. It will help you to use your mental body more effectively, too. Once you connect your thoughts with your emotions you will begin to direct your lives with more joy. You will feel, not just think, the power you have. Whether you are in a male body or a female body, it has physical, mental, emotional, and spiritual components. The instructions for how to get your body to perform at its best are the same whether you are male or female.

L. I bet a lot of people will have a hard time with that. There is a lot of information out now about how different men are from women.

G. Yes, causing much confusion. On the surface it appears to be of help. And of course it is. But surface help only goes that far. If you continually look at each other as separate and different, you will continue to miss each other.

At your core, your essence, you are all the same.

You are all love—female or male, it matters not. As a soul in a female body, you will have different experiences than a soul in a male body. But it is time for each of you to go to your core.

The time has come for all people to open up to heart energy.

No matter whether your experience is from a female body or a male body, you are seeking to know love. And love is love is love is love is love. Love is! Love is female. Love is male. Love is neither. Love is both. Love is all. Love is! You are love. I am love. Know love. Come from love in all that you do, and you will not have to be concerned with male and female.

L. How nice that would be! I can understand it where my son is concerned. And my clients. It is amazing to me how alike we all are.

G. Feelings and heart energy are linked. Emotions are tools within the emotional body, tools that are meant to be used by you. Your emotions are not meant to use you. You are in charge of your emotions, just as you are in charge of your thoughts. The heart energy that you feel is opening you to the tools that you have within, allowing you to create and experience the life you desire.

L. Please explain the connection between feelings and intuition.

G. Feelings are the body's way of giving you information. Your body is your greatest ally. It is your vehicle, your

way of experiencing the physical world. You have all that
you need within you. Feelings are sensations you experience in your body that give you direct information about
what you are experiencing. If you are in danger, your body
lets you know. If something you hear is true, your body
lets you know. If something isn't right, your body lets you
know. Intuition is part of this "feeling" system. It is time
you honored the feelings that you have. You can trust these
feelings. They are always acting in your interest. Intuition
has several names. "Gut feeling" is one of the most popu-
lar. Intuition comes from heart energy.

L. How does it connect with intuition?

G. Heart energy is directly linked to your spirit. And, of course,
your soul speaks to you through your spirit, which you
hear through your heart or emotional body. You cannot
hear your soul speak to you through your mental body.
You have learned much about your physical body and your
mental body. You have long ignored your heart and spirit.
It is time to learn how you can use your heart and spirit to
fulfill your soul's journey. You are here for a reason. You
are here to learn who you are. Heart energy will open you
up to the depths of your being. Heart energy opens you up
to the frequency of love.

**Heart energy enables you to experience love at a deep
level.**

L. How will we experience heart energy? What effect will it
have on us?

G. You will notice that you are using emotions that in the past
you may not have allowed yourself to experience fully.

There will be a depth and spontaneity to your experience that you haven't felt before. Situations will arise in your lives in which you will respond from your heart instead of your head. You are already realizing that you create your life through your heart. It is a powerful tool at your disposal. You will discover that your heart has answers that your head can not comprehend.

Highlights

1. All people are opening up to heart energy.

2. Feelings and heart energy are linked.

3. Feelings are the body's way of giving you information from your spirit.

4. Heart energy is directly linked to your spirit.

5. Your soul speaks to you through your spirit, which you hear through your heart.

6. Heart energy opens you to the frequency of love.

7. With heart energy, you will find a new depth and spontaneity in your experience.

8. You will discover that your heart has answers that your head cannot comprehend.

18

Energy

G. What is wrong with you today?

L. I just feel blocked, as if the flow of energy has stopped. I feel stuck.

G. Linda, Linda, Linda!

L. Oh, oh. I know that tone. You are not pleased with me.

G. It's not that I'm not pleased with you. It's that *you* are not pleased with you. And what did you learn blocks energy?

L. Fear! But I don't feel afraid.

G. Fear comes in many, many disguises. It doesn't always feel the same. Except for something that always gives it away.

L. What is that? How can we know we are in fear?

G. What did you just say about how you were feeling?

L. I said that I was feeling blocked, as if my energy has stopped flowing.

G. And what did we say fear is?

L. Energy that is blocked or scattered.

G. Very good! Now we're getting somewhere. Remember, fear

also has a purpose. Do you remember what we said about the two kinds of fear?

L. Yes! There is the fear that comes when we are in danger from an outside source, and there is the fear that comes in moments of opportunity.

G. Very good. Now are you in danger from an outside source?

L. No. At least, I don't think so.

G. Linda, you know! Trust yourself. You are playing games now. Are you in danger from an outside source?

L. No! The danger is from within. Fear is the danger.

G. That's right. You are in a moment of opportunity, are you not?

L. Yes! But this is getting confusing!

G. Confusing! *Au contraire!* We are clarifying the feeling that you are experiencing. You said that you were feeling blocked. The energy isn't flowing. Why might the energy be blocked? This is a moment of opportunity. Fear comes in many disguises. Where is the first place you tell people to look when their energy is blocked?

L. Look to the chief feature, the trap!

G. That's it! What is your chief feature?

L. Impatience!

G. And how are you feeling? Say a little bit more about what is going on with you.

L. Well, I am feeling a bit rushed, like I have a lot of things to do. My mind keeps jumping to other things that I have to do today. And of course my energy feels stuck and scattered at the same time. It just isn't flowing like it usually does.

G. And how does impatience feel?

L. Okay, I see what you mean. I just described how impatience feels in the body. Boy, it sure can be subtle! I didn't think I was in fear or in my chief feature.

G. Thinking won't help you here, unless you use it to guide your mental body to the process that will help you direct your energy. Your mental body can go all over the place. And if you are in fear, where do you think it will go if there is no guidance from you?

L. I see now. Of course it will go down the path of fear. If I don't guide it to another direction, it will continue down the path it is on! This is great! I am understanding more and more how important it is for us to be in charge of our thoughts. To be aware of what we are thinking and the path we are choosing to follow.

G. That's right, Linda! Speaking of thoughts and the paths you are following, how did you move into fear in the first place? How did you get caught in the trap of your chief feature?

L. I'm not so sure I want to know how I got stuck!

G. Why not? Do it from observation mode. Judge not . . .

Linda, it will help you to be able to see the connection between what you are thinking and how it affects your energy. Once you understand the different ways you change your energy, you will be more careful and aware of what you are thinking and doing. All that you think becomes who you are.

L. Thank you! I'll go into observation mode. So, what I have been thinking has affected my energy, causing it to be blocked as well as scattered?

Energy

G. Yes! And what have you have been discussing? And what people have you been around? Remember, you can pick up on other people's energy.

L. When I am picking up on other people's energy, is there anything I can do to stay in love and not move into the fear that they may be in?

G. Yes, there are things you can do. Yet you must understand that all is one. What touches one, touches all. Energy has no boundaries. When you open your energy, allowing it to flow freely, you create a space for anyone near you to open their energy. On a grander scale, you create a space for the whole to flow freely.

L. Does that mean that if one person's energy is blocked, it affects us all?

G. Yes.

L. But doesn't that make for quite an impossible situation? No wonder we feel so out of control. If just one person can affect my energy, what can I do?

G. **You are either taking in information or sending it out. Information provides the basis for change.**

L. Wait a minute, I thought you said that our thoughts change our energy. Or even our breathing.

G. And what are thoughts but information?

L. Yes, of course that makes sense. What about breathing?

G. Your breath is perhaps your greatest source of information. Breathe in what you desire, breathe out what you don't want. You can breathe in the energy of love and confidence, you can breathe out the energy of fear and doubt.

Your breathing tells you much. Why do you think doctors check your breathing all the time? It certainly isn't just to see if you are alive. They are gathering "information."

L. So we are either taking in information or sending it out?

G. Yes!

L. Does that mean we are always supposed to be sending out information so that we won't pick up on someone else's thoughts?

G. Yes and no!

L. Oh, oh, here we go again! Please explain.

G. Yes, you are always sending out information. And no, not so that you won't be picking up on someone else's thoughts but so that you will be aware of what you are tuning into. You are all part of the whole. You are not alone. You need each other. Each one of you has a piece of the puzzle.

You are meant to share the information you have. And you are meant to learn from each other.

L. Go on!

G. Each of you has free will. You get to live in love or fear, as you please. You get to rediscover who you are as quickly or as slowly as you desire. You get to experience as much hardship or as much joy as you wish. Each of you has your own path, your own way. But the destination is the same. And it matters not how long it takes you to get there or which route you take. You will all arrive.

L. So it is a matter of how we choose to get there. And where is it we are going again?

G. Home!

L. Home? And where is home?

Energy

G. I am home. I am here. I am there. I am.

L. How can I possibly understand that you are here, and you are there, and you are everywhere? I am not even sure I know who you are or even that you are!

G. Well, that is a bit amusing, wouldn't you say? Do you always go around talking to someone who isn't there?

L. How can I possibly understand God?

G. Love! Through love. The way to God is through love. Know love, and you know God.

L. Wow! It is always about love.

G. Yes, it is.

L. All right! This does feel better. Can we get back to our discussion on energy? How do we control the taking in of energy?

G. If you don't want to be in someone else's fear . . .or rather I could say it another way:

If you don't want to go down someone else's path, stay on your own path. If you are with someone, or even thinking about someone, you are tuning into their energy.

This is how your energy system, your body, works. It is an important part of how you pick up on information. It is how you gather information.

L. So, what if we don't want the information that is being sent out?

G. You can reject it. It's simple. You always have a choice. You are always choosing your path. Where you are going is your decision. You get to write your own story.

L. How can we reject energy? Sometimes, it seems like I have no control over that.

G. Most of the time you have complete control over what you are taking in and what you are refusing. It is true that sometimes you feel overwhelmed by the energy coming your way. By the fear. But that is only an illusion. That is only fear in disguise. You always have a choice to come from fear or to come from love.

L. Is feeling overwhelmed an emotion?

G. Yes, it certainly is. It explains the sensation you feel when taking in a lot of energy from different sources all at once. It can also be a blocking emotion. When you have much to do, you may choose "overwhelm" so that you don't have to do anything. Of course you don't consciously say that to yourself. But that is the purpose of overwhelm—to stop all action. So if you use it, you must know its purpose or function. Ignorance of its function will not excuse you from its results.

L. But what about all the bad things that happen in life over which we have no control?

G. You are getting lost again. Lost in your body as you.

You are not your body. You are love. You are having an experience in a body. You are not your body. When you can truly understand this, you will understand what freedom is. And that you are always creating your life. The situations you find yourself in are not who you are. They are merely opportunities for you to express more and more of who you truly are.

L. And that is?

G. Linda, you are love.

L. I know. But sometimes I just seem to get lost in the details of my life. I get lost in what is happening to me, in what is surrounding me. In what I am supposed to be doing!

G. And what are you supposed to be doing?

L. Well, I have all these calls to make. I want to work out. I am meeting with the tennis team this afternoon. Things like that.

G. What is happening to your energy? How do you feel?

L. Rushed. Like I don't have enough time to do everything. I want to keep writing, too.

G. You are moving quickly into fear. Your energy is starting to get scattered. Earlier it was blocked. Now, it is scattering. What can you do to move back into free-flowing energy?

L. Practice what I am preaching?

G. Yes, exactly! And what are you preaching?

L. Love!

G. So how can you come from love in the situation you are facing?

L. I'm not sure where to begin.

G. You want more specific instructions. That is fair. After all, that is what this book is about.

Here are instructions to regain your flow of energy:

1. **Take a deep breath**. Allow yourself a moment to collect your energy. You will be gathering information as you breathe in. You don't need to know what you are gathering. Just trust that it will be the information you need in this moment. Turning your attention to your

breathing will bring you into the present moment. Do it! Take a deep breath. In fact, take a couple of deep breaths. How are you feeling?

L. It feels good just to breathe.

G. Deep breathing will help to center you. When you are centered you are in the present moment. When you are in the present moment, right action is always possible. You will hear your soul's guidance in this moment. This is what it is about. Now,

2. **Listen**! Listen to the guidance of your soul. What is it telling you to do?

L. I think it is telling me to stop writing for now.

G. Don't think—but feel and listen! What is it telling you to do?

L. To stop! We have made a lot of progress, and some good points have come from it. It's time now to move on to other tasks.

G. So stop we shall!

Highlights

1. Energy that is either blocked or scattered comes from fear.

2. When your energy is blocked or scattered, look to the chief feature.

3. Without guidance, fear will continue down the path of fear.

4. Connect your thinking with your energy.

5. What touches one touches all. Energy has no boundaries.

6. Your breath is perhaps your greatest source of information.

7. We are either taking in information, or sending it out.

8. The destination is the same for everyone—home!

9. If you are thinking of someone, you are tuning into their energy.

10. You always have a choice to come from fear or to come from love.

11. You are not your body. You are love.

12. The situations you find yourself in are opportunities for you to express the love that you are.

13. Take a deep breath and listen. Listen to your soul's guidance.

19

Create Your Day with "Hows"

G. This is your day! Create it as you desire. This is your day, woman! Make it the kind of day you want to create! Now! Create! Tell me the kind of day you would like. Your wish is my command!

L. This is fun! Okay! I'd like to spend a couple of hours writing and talking with you. I'd like to get the energy flowing again. I want this book to be written well. I want the information to be helpful to all those open to its valuable information. I want to help people.

Then, I want to spend a little bit of time working on my house repairs, spend the afternoon working with the tennis team, and tonight I want to go to a movie and for a walk.

G. Linda, stop! How do you want to express who you are? You have some control over the details of your day. Some. But as you have noticed, the details seem to change, and you don't always have control over what happens in a day. But who you are and how you express who you are is always within your control.

Create Your Day with "Hows"

It is important how you express the who that you are, not the "whats" in your life.

The what is there only to allow you an opportunity to express more and more of who you are.

L. You are right! We get lost in the what, don't we? What we have. What we don't have. What we want. What we don't want. What others have. What others have that we don't have. What is happening. What isn't happening. The situations we find ourselves in. The problems we create. The challenges we face. The people in our lives. The people who aren't in our lives. The relationship we want. The relationship we don't want . . .

G. And what else Linda? What are some of the other whats that you get lost in?

L. Health. That's a big one. When I'm not feeling well, it can pretty much take over everything in my life.

G. As well it does for many people. But this is no different from anything else in your life.

L. What do you mean? It certainly feels a lot different. What are we supposed to do? I know I didn't like it when I wasn't feeling well not too long ago. And I don't like it when I feel stiff or my energy is low. What are we supposed to do?

G. Again, Linda, it isn't the what. It is the how! How you express who you are in any situation.

L. You make me smile! I feel your presence with me today.

G. And have you not felt my presence other days?

L. No, not every day. I have to admit I haven't.

G. Why is that, my child?

L. It is so interesting. I can feel the tenderness in your voice. I can feel differences in you.

G. Of course you can! Did you not think that I, too, have many expressions?

L. Well, actually, I had never thought of it that way. You were always something, or someone, that I only felt at certain times. And I didn't really know you like I am getting to know you now. There is so much more to you than I ever imagined. Please show yourself.

G. How will you know that it is I?

L. You could do some grand miracle.

G. The sun rising and setting every day is not miracle enough?

L. Yes! But you know what I mean. Something out of the ordinary.

G. Okay.

L. Okay what?

G. Remember it is not the what in life but the how. How you express who you are defines who you are. It creates your story. It is your life. Your day is filled either with love or with fear. Which do you choose?

L. Well, love, of course.

G. Of course!

L. But back to the miracle.

G. Open your eyes, open your ears. Allow yourself to see. Allow yourself to hear. Allow yourself to feel. I am. Believe in miracles! Know that I am. You will see me in all that you see.

L. No, I want something that proves you exist. I want to know you.

G. You do know me. You are getting lost in your society's description of God as man. God is in all that is. Until you are willing to let go of your answers as to who or what I am, you will not be able to know me. You will not be able to see me. You will not be able to experience the "I am" that I am.

L. There is a huge part of me that understands. And when I am in love, when I am coming from my heart, I know.

G. Now, you have it! That's why heart energy is so important.

L. It is how we come to know God!

G. Yes, you have it, my dear. You finally have it! You cannot experience God with your head. You cannot "think" God. You know God through your heart. And that cannot be explained in words. You will get lost in the kind of confusion that only your thoughts can bring about. Stay in your heart. Listen to your heart. Your heart is the messenger of your soul.

L. It feels so good to hear you say that. I know that what you say is true.

G. Always! Of course! So, you see, it is not the what that matters. Why have you not felt my presence always?

L. I guess it is because I haven't taken the time to be silent. To go to that place inside of me where I feel love. I have been too busy with the what of my life.

G. Do you know where you go when you are stuck in the what of life?

L. Fear?

G. Yes, fear. You lose sight of who you are and how you want to express the love that you are. What are some of the other whats that you get lost in?

L. Beauty! Beauty is a what that traps most of us.

G. Yes! Men get trapped in the beauty myth. More than women. Did you know that?

L. No! As a matter of fact, I think it is the other way around. Women get trapped in fashion and cosmetics.

G. Well, perhaps we are both right. Men and women get trapped. And neither has much luck escaping the trap as long as they stay stuck in the what.

L. Please explain the what of the beauty myth.

G. Oh, Linda. That is obvious, is it not? Have you not heard yourself ask, "What does he look like?" Or heard others ask, "What does she look like?" or "What are you going to wear?" Beauty—what a person looks like or what a person wears—does not make the person.

L. It seems to have a lot of influence on us.

G. That is another way you have lost your way. Do you realize how much time and energy you spend on what you look like? And in the end, does it matter all that much? When you are making love, is it what your lover looks like that you are experiencing, or the love that is your lover? And in the other relationships in your life? Does it matter at all to you what your son or daughter looks like? Or to them, what you look like? Doesn't the child love the parent unconditionally? Have you not felt the purity of this love? When you have been with Josh and Lisa, have those moments not been filled with love? Yes, because you were filled with love. You were in your heart. You were expressing who you truly are. Therein lies true beauty.

Uncover the myth. Release yourself from this myth, and see your life transformed. The energy you will gain from releasing the need to be "beautiful" will astonish you. You will have more energy than you ever had.

It will be easier for you to come from love. The beauty thing has caused more problems for you than you can imagine. What would your life be like if you came from love in all your interactions with others and with yourself? If you let go of the need or desire to be beautiful? Do it for just one day. See how much better and easier your life will be.

All of you are beautiful. You will begin to see that clearly. You will no longer buy into industry beauty. Stereotypes! Guide your mind to see only beauty in all that you see.

L. I can see your point that every*one* is beautiful, but every*thing* is not beautiful. There is a lot of ugliness in the world. Ugliness and cruelty. How can that be beautiful?

G. In your world, in the world you are creating, you can see beauty in all of God's creations. Yes, it is true that people choose different paths back to love. But it is all about love. You are love. See the love and YOUR life will be one of love. Live in fear, live in illusion, and your life will be one of fear and illusion. It can be no other way.

See fear, and you are fear. See love, and you are love.

L. I'm getting lost again. Are you telling us to ignore all the cruelty and injustices in the world? That doesn't seem right.

G. No, I am not telling you to ignore all the cruelty and injustices in the world. I am telling you to come from love in all that you do. Be the love that you are. You cannot go wrong in love.

L. You had better explain that.

G. When you come from love, your actions will be right action. You will know what to do and you will do it. Easily and naturally. That is all. Life happens. What you do is not important. The expression of who you are in each and every moment is important. One person's right may be another person's wrong. Who is to say who is right? You are both right. You are both coming from who you are. How can it be anything but right. Remember, this is your soul's journey. No one else can tell you what is right for you. You must listen to your own inner guidance to discover what is right for you.

If there is a what to be concerned with, it is the what of your soul's journey.

L. So if I feel that correcting what I perceive to be an injustice is what I am supposed to do, I'll do it. But what if murdering someone is what I feel is my soul's path?

G. Then you will do it.

L. Now wait a minute. I know murder is wrong!

G. And what would you do if someone were attacking your son and the only way to stop that person from harming your son would be to shoot him? Would you do it?

L. Yes, I know I would do anything to save him.

G. Didn't you say murder was wrong?

L. That wouldn't be murder!

G. Oh? Are you not taking the life of another? Do you have that right?

L. Yes, to protect my son, I do!

G. Who is to say what you are doing is right and what someone else is doing is wrong?

L. That is obvious. Everyone can see that!

G. I can tell you that the person who murders someone on the street for what appears to you no reason at all is not different from you murdering someone to save your son.

L. No way! How can you say that? God would never say that!

G. Are you saying that I'm not God?

L.   Well, it doesn't sound very godlike.

G.   Oh, Linda! Are you so lost? Go to your heart.

L.   I know that you are God. But some of these answers are pretty tough to understand.

G.   All you can do, all anyone can do, is live from your truth. Live from the love that you are. You cannot control what anyone else does with their life. You can make laws, yes. You can lock people up in prisons, yes. But you cannot live anyone else's life for them. Each of you must come from your truth. When you are not coming from your truth, is when you feel lost.

L.   I know what you are saying. I have been studying how to come from love and fear for a long time.

G.   Interesting! You are indeed an interesting young woman!

L.   Young! You make me sound so naive.

G.   And are you not naive? You are wise, it is true. But you have much to learn, have you not?

L.   Oh, yes. I know that is true. Sometimes I am amazed at all I know. Other times I am amazed at how little I know.

G.   Which brings us to another what that distracts people.

L.   What is that?

G.   Age, of course!

L.   Oh, yes! This is a good topic.

G.   We are going to save that for another time. It is time for you to move.

L.   I was beginning to notice my energy moving elsewhere. But I would really like to keep writing. It seems like we are getting somewhere, and I don't want to stop.

G.   All in good time. All in good time. Remember, it isn't what you are doing—but how you are doing it.

Highlights

1. This is your day! Create it as you desire!

2. Who you are and how you express who you are is always in your control.

3. You cannot experience God with your head but through your heart.

4. Beauty is another "what" trap.

5. Beauty is found in the expression of who you truly are.

6. The energy you gain from releasing the need to be beautiful will astonish you.

7. Guide your mind to see the beauty within everyone you meet.

8. Be the love that you are.

9. What you do is not important. The expression of who you are in each and every moment is important.

20

Embracing Life

L. I don't know what happened yesterday, but writing was just not in the day's plans.

G. And you honored the energy. You didn't force it. That is good work. How was your day?

L. It went very well. Chanda came out to my home for a private session. She is doing very well. All of the soul-searching and work that she did last year is paying off this year. She is more at peace with herself. She feels good about herself and what she is doing with her life and with her tennis.

G. What was one of the topics you covered with her?

L. Self-image, as a matter of fact. We talked about how she sees herself on the tennis court. What kind of athlete she is. What kind of friend she is. In fact, we got into all the different roles she has and how she can create her own story by being who she wants to be in each of these roles.

G. That is a good topic.

Being in a body allows you the opportunity to create yourself in a variety of different situations, roles.

    Understanding this basic concept will take you a long way toward living in peace in a body.

L. Why is that so hard for us to take advantage of?

G. Because you have not been taught how to use your inner tools correctly, you have the impression that you have no control over who you are. Using your inner tools incorrectly creates frustration and disillusionment within you. You think that, no matter what you do, ultimately it doesn't matter, that you don't have control over all you create in your life. Taking it to the extreme, you feel as if there is no hope. You are doomed to a life of misery and worry. Or a life of illness and discomfort in your body. That just isn't so. That is not the framework of the body. You are meant to live in your body however you desire. You can live in joy. You can embrace life. Or you can live in misery. How you use your body, your whole body, determines the path you are on.

L. So what you are saying is that if we use our tools and our bodies incorrectly, or not as they were meant to be used, we will feel out of control because, in effect, we are out of control!

G. That is it exactly! You are out of control, so of course you feel out of control! Imagine yourself riding a beautiful thoroughbred horse. You are told that this horse can take you wherever you want to go. It is a special horse. It can fly. Fly not only in this dimension, but into other dimensions as well.

L. Oh! That would be so cool! I love horses!
G. Yes! But in your excitement to get on this horse, you for-
    get to ask how to guide the horse to where you want to go.
    At first, you are riding along, enjoying the beautiful scen-
    ery and the flow of movement and energy on this body of
    horse. But after awhile you decide you want to go in a
    different direction. You want a change, but you don't know
    how to get the horse to turn. It goes on and on in the same
    direction. And now it even speeds up. You go faster and
    faster towards what you don't want. You begin to feel a bit
    frantic, a bit out of control. You pull and tug and kick the
    horse to no avail. The horse only gets angry and goes all
    the faster. Now, the smooth ride no longer feels so smooth.
    It is getting bumpy, uncomfortable. You begin to swear at
    the horse. What a rotten horse this is! It is no good! It won't
    do what I tell it to do! Meanwhile your horse is turning
    this way and that way with every pull and tug on the reins.
    Whereas before the horse was gentle and efficient in all its
    movements, it is now rough and looking more and more
    tortured with each step.

        You no longer know what to do. You begin to think
    there is something definitely wrong with the horse. Your
    dream of exploring other dimensions seems an impossible
    dream. You wonder how you could have thought it was
    possible in the first place. The ride goes on for so long in
    that manner that you start to get used to the ride. The dis-
    comfort starts feeling normal. You are going so fast that
    you no longer notice the guideposts along the way. You
    don't even realize that there are guideposts.

        Yet you keep searching for the way. You search and
    search for something on the outside. You know you have

to keep looking until you find it. You have moments when you feel that if you stop everything will come crumbling down around you. At other moments the fear is so strong you find yourself in a cold sweat. Still you ride on and on. Your horse is getting weaker and weaker. Instead of stopping to give it some recovery time and to refuel, you forge on. Life is meant to be tough. You just have to be tough yourself. You just have to keep going. You don't stop and reevaluate where you are. You are getting somewhere. Where? Where are you getting?

L. No where?

G. Nowhere! Because you don't know how to guide your horse, it is going off here and there, not really going anywhere. You feel out of control. You are out of control as long as you ride a horse you don't know how to ride. You are in a body. Your body is how you get around. It can take you anywhere. It can take you into other dimensions. You just need instructions. Follow these instructions, and you will get where you want to go.

You can choose from different paths. All you need to do is look a little ways down the path. You will easily see where you are headed. Is it where you want to go?

L. But sometimes even when we don't like where we are headed, we can't seem to change paths.

G. Only because you use your inner tools incorrectly. Or you don't use them at all. Your body is a fine piece of work. Never underestimate what it can do. You say you can't fly in a body? Look at a gymnast flying through the air. Your acclaimed athletes demonstrate beautifully for you what your body can do. Just because you choose not to do what it takes for your body to fly, does not mean that it can't. You know that airplanes can fly, right?

L. Yes, of course! They were created to fly.

G. You were created to fly. One day you will know this. For now, you are satisfied taking airplanes for your flight. Still, some people among you are using inner planes for their flight. Too often you judge your body as being inadequate when, with no training or practice, it can't do something you want it to do. Can you touch your toes?

L. You mean bend over and touch my toes? No.

G. Yes, you can! You just need to practice and stretch regularly, and you will be able to do it easily. You only say no because you are not doing what it takes for your body to be able to bend freely at this time. Not because your body can't do it but because you are not doing what it takes for it to be able to do it. It has nothing to do with age. Young and old bodies alike have been created to bend and stretch freely. They just must to do it consistently to maintain the ability.

Remember that your physical body has needs. One of its needs is movement. If you give it movement on a regular basis, it will help you to stay healthy and strong for a lifetime.

L. **So as we learn how to use our inner tools correctly, we will be able to create the lives we desire.**

G. Yes. Your soul is on a journey. There is no stopping the journey. All is part of the journey.

L. The journey to ourselves. To God. To love . . .

G. Yes, to love. A wonderful journey, is it not?

L. Well, that depends!

G. Yes, depends on the choices you make. On the path you decide to take. It is true that life happens. That is what life is. A series of happenings. Stop for five minutes, just five minutes every day. Be silent. Allow yourself to hear your inner guidance. Hear your soul's message. Hear the guidance your soul is broadcasting at all times.

In this silence you will hear this message, and you will know who you are. From this place of knowing you will then begin to live and create your life.

You will notice that what is happening on the outside isn't what matters. What is happening on the inside matters. Always.

L. Okay. I have a question for you. It is a cold, dreary day out. I want to go to a movie, but it looks so cold outside. How can I get myself to go out in the cold?

G. This is an easy one for you. Where does creation in a body begin?

L. In thought. Yes! In thought. Everything is first created in thought and then in the material world.

G. That is right. So, what can you do to get your body outside today?

L. I change my thought about it. Instead of thinking it is too cold and dreary out. I think, "Today, I am going to 'do cold.' I am coming from love, so it doesn't matter what is happening on the outside. I am love. Whether it is cold or hot doesn't matter." I can start thinking about how much fun it will be to go to a movie. I can start thinking about how easy it will be to "do cold" today.

G. Which tools do you need to accomplish this?

L. Discipline, to guide my thoughts down the path of joy rather than the path of misery.

G. Good. Now what else?

L. Enthusiasm, to fuel my physical body to move to get dressed for outside.

G. All right! You have the idea. Is there anything else you could use?

L. Yes, appreciation! I can use appreciation to help me see how lucky I am that I can even go to a movie. I just talked to a dear friend of mine who isn't feeling well enough to do anything but go to the doctor. She would love to be able to go to a movie or for a walk but now isn't able. Imagine not being able to move your body the way you would like to move it. Whenever I think I am too tired to exercise, I think about how lucky I am to be able to work out. It has an amazing effect on me. Rarely do I skip workouts when I think this way. It is motivating.

Highlights

1. Honor your energy.

2. Being in a body allows you the opportunity to create yourself in a variety of different situations.

3. Using your inner tools incorrectly creates frustration and disillusionment within you.

4. You can live in joy, or you can live in misery—the choice is always yours.

5. Hear your inner guidance. Hear your soul's messages.

6. Decide what you want, and choose the correct inner tool to help you achieve it.

21

The Power of Belief

L.   I love my life! I had the most wonderful weekend.

G.   Appreciation is always good for the soul! So, what was so wonderful about your weekend?

L.   I was with the tennis team at a tournament. There were many things going on with each one of the four young women who were playing from our team.

G.   What questions do you have about what happened?

L.   I don't totally understand what happened with Martina in her semifinal match.

G.   Tell us what the situation was.

L.   Okay. Martina prepared very well for the match. We talked a lot over the few days we were there. I explained how she needed to use her inner tools to help her body perform at higher levels. We even did a session together the night before her semifinal match. I thought she understood. She had done so well in her earlier matches. Why didn't it work in this match?

G. Linda, did she really do what you told her to do? In the earlier matches, did she do it on her own, or did you have to help her?

L. No, I guess she didn't do everything. But her preparation was so good. I don't understand.

G. Patience, Linda. Let's go over it some more. We've talked about Martina before. What happened to her in her match?

L. She froze. Her energy was stuck. She walked as if she could hardly lift her feet. She was stuck in a thought pattern.

G. What thought pattern did you see?

L. "I have to win this match. My whole career is at stake. I'm so nervous. If I lose, I lose everything."

G. How did that affect her physically?

L. She could hardly move. Her energy was almost totally blocked. Everything she did was off. She couldn't hit her volleys. Her forehand was weak. It wasn't her game at all.

G. As we discussed earlier, when your energy is stuck your body cannot move and perform as it normally does. You know all of this, Linda. What is your question?

L. Why couldn't I help her?

G. You did help her.

L. No, I mean help her move her energy. Why didn't what I was telling her to do work?

G. You can only help her. You can't do it for her.

L. But other times it seemed like I was helping her to move her energy.

G. Yes, and you were. But she has to be open. And she has to believe in herself. Belief is one of your most powerful tools.

In the earlier matches, she believed in herself. In this match, it was different.

L. How was it different?

G. What thought pattern did you say she was stuck in?

L. "I have to win or I lose everything. My whole career depends on this match."

G. Can you now see the difference between this match and the earlier matches? In her earlier matches, she was playing one match at a time. In any one match, she believes in herself. But in the match to decide whether or not she would go to Dallas, she played as if her entire career were at stake. She was not playing one match, but all of her matches in one. Does she believe she can make it on the tour? That is where she lacks belief, does she not?

L. Yes. She told me she doesn't know whether she can make it.

G. And there you have it. Belief is necessary to accomplish your dreams, your goals.

L. Are you saying that if she had believed in herself, she would have won that match?

G. No! Of course not! That is not the essence of the game. Winning or losing is not what we are talking about here. Is your concern about the fact that she didn't win?

L. No. It is about how she played.

G. Yes, Linda!

Life is about how you live—not about what you have, or even what you do. Life is about how you express who you are.

How you create your life. That is what life is. That is what it is always about. How did Martina play? Or I could say, how did she live her life in those moments during her match?

L. Fear. She was expressing herself from fear. That is why she was stuck. She was in fear. But before the match she seemed okay. What happened?

G. She thought about how she had to win. It triggered the thought pattern we discussed. Remember, your thoughts fuel your emotional body. She chose fear through the thoughts she chose. Her body was forced to respond to the process. Instead of belief, she chose doubt. It is as simple as that. And as complicated.

L. But why couldn't I help her as I was able to do earlier?

G. You did help her. Accept the result.

L. That she lost?

G. No. That she couldn't move out of doubt.

Belief is powerful—in the negative as well as in the positive.

She believed she couldn't do it. Remember, it wasn't about just this match. She knew she beat the woman she was playing in previous matches. She already had beaten her two out of three times. She wasn't playing against her, though. She was playing against all of her doubts, all of her fears that she isn't good enough. Belief is meant to be powerful. It has a force about it that is meant to move mountains. Therefore, you cannot change beliefs over night. Inherent in beliefs is their strength. They are meant to be strong, difficult to change. If they were easy to change, you would change them every time you came up against an obstacle.

L. I get it. Martina's belief that she isn't good enough came up against an obstacle.

G. That's right. What was the obstacle?

L. That she was good enough. She had played this girl before and had beaten her. If she won, that would mean that she could make it on the tour—in her mind, anyway. But of course she couldn't do that because that would go against her belief that she isn't good enough to be on the tour.

G. Exactly. The obstacle was the real possibility of winning. The power of her belief took over.

L. Was there anything I could have done?

G. No. You did everything you could do. Belief in yourself is a private thing. You can believe in her. That does help, of course. You can give her reasons to believe in herself. Eventually, it always comes down to the individual. Belief is personal. You can do it only for yourself. Just like all of your tools, in the end it is up to each individual to make the choice.

L. So what does Martina have to do? How do you dissolve one belief and choose another?

G. Belief is a verb. Yes, it then turns into a noun. What we are talking about now is the tool belief. This is something you use. Just like confidence, trust, joy and so on. You believe. The way you choose belief is by believing.

L. Yes, but how?

225

G. Okay . . . **This is how you choose and use an inner tool.**

1. **Awareness.** Know which tool you are choosing.
2. **Take a deep breath and think thoughts that believe in you.** For instance: "I believe in myself. I can play on the tour. I can do it. I want to do it. I deserve success. I believe in my ability. I trust my training. I trust myself. I believe in myself. I work hard. I know what I am doing. I am an athlete."
3. **Live your life in tune with this belief.** In every moment, discipline your thoughts to thoughts of belief in yourself. Do whatever action you must to reach your goal. Begin now to act as if your goal has been achieved. Think about what you would do differently if you already had achieved your goal. How would you play if you were already on the tour? How would you train? What would you eat? Things like that.
4. **Choose to believe in yourself.** Choice is powerful. Choose belief over and over again.
5. **Trust.** Trust that as long as you stay on the path that leads you to your goal, you will reach it.

Belief is not a tool that lends itself to changing direction. If your belief is that you aren't good enough, you will have to do some inner work to dissolve this belief and create a new one. The work you do, Linda, with your clients will be vital in this process. Taking them to their essence, their core, is the fastest way to dissolve old beliefs and create new ones.

L. Okay, let me make sure I have this straight. To bring out one of our inner tools, we must be aware of what we want, breathe in the energy of the tool, act on our choice, trust that it is happening and be sure we are choosing this tool over and over again.

G. That's it.

L. It sounds simple, but Martina sure had trouble drawing it out on Saturday.

G. Again I will tell you that belief is different from the other tools. Because of its nature, it does not change directions easily. But once you experience the power of belief, you will be eager to use it in your life.

L. I know that is true for me. There have been many times when I was the only one who believed in what I was doing. I know that if I hadn't believed in myself and that I could do anything I put my mind to, I would never have started this book.

G. Yes, Linda. Your belief is what allowed you to hear me.

L. It is incredible. Will the world ever be a place of love?

G. It already is a place of love. Do you not feel it? Do you not see it in your son's look? In your friend's touch? In your heart?

Highlights

1. When your energy is stuck or scattered, your body can't move and perform as it normally does.

2. Belief is one of your most powerful tools.

3. You can help others move their energy, but you can't do it for them.

4. Belief is necessary to accomplish your dreams and goals.

5. Doubt blocks your energy, while belief moves you forward with strength.

6. Your thoughts change your energy.

7. Inherent in belief is strength.

8. Beliefs are not meant to be changed easily.

9. Belief is a private thing.

10. You can dissolve one belief and choose another through:

    • Awareness of what you want
    • Living your life in tune with the new belief
    • Choosing to believe in yourself
    • Using your breath and thoughts.

22

Confusion and Denial

L. God? Are you there?

G. Good-morning, Linda. Do you still doubt that I am here?

L. No, of course not! I am just not sure how to address God!

G. What else is bothering you?

L. I didn't say that anything is bothering me!

G. And do you think you have to say anything for me to know?

L. No, I guess not. I don't know what is bothering me. This reminds me of when I talk to some of the athletes I work with. I seem to know something is bothering them before they do. Sometimes, it doesn't sit too well with them that I see something is bothering them—and they don't. They're polite, but I can tell they are annoyed. Why is that? Am I wrong? I know something is bothering them. I can see it in their energy fields. Yet wouldn't they know?

G. They do know. They may not be ready to acknowledge it.

L. Why is that?

G. Because once you acknowledge what is bothering you, you can't hide in "I don't know" or in denial. You feel compelled to take action to change it.

L. Why would we want to hide in confusion or denial? That doesn't make sense!

G. Of course it makes sense. It makes perfect sense. It is your body's way of giving you time to accept what is going on, to find another way, to find an answer, or to prepare yourself for the next step. But there always comes a time to move on, to continue in the flow of life's energy. It is when you refuse or are unaware of this flow of life that the body feels the sensation of annoyance, frustration, or even anger. This is your sign that it is time to move on. To do something about what is happening in your life.

L. And if we refuse?

G. More annoyance, frustration, and anger!

L. What then? Eventually we have to move on, right?

G. Not necessarily! There is another choice.

L. What other choice?

G. To turn it inward. It is one of the ways you create disease in your body. You hold onto experiences instead of allowing them to become a part of the fabric of your life. Instead of blessing them, you condemn them. Instead of accepting them, you judge them.

L. What are we supposed to do with them? I don't think anyone enjoys being stuck. It's easy to say, "Get on with it." But doing it is another story.

G. Is it? Why do you say one choice is harder than another?

L. Well it is, of course. What are you saying?

G. And it is so easy to stay in your confusion, your misery? Being bothered? Being annoyed? Being angry? You find this an easier choice?

L. I see what you mean. So why do we find it so hard to let go? To move on? To flow with life's energy?

G. Because you have not been taught how to do this. You have been taught how to stay in your confusion but not how to move out of it.

L. How have we been taught to stay in our confusion? I don't remember ever being taught that kind of thing!

G. By example. It is your greatest teacher. You see other people doing it one way, and you imitate them. Do you remember my telling you that sport is meant to show you how to use your inner tools? How to stay in the flow?

L. This is so weird, but I get it. I see what you are saying about sport now.

G. Yes, it is one of your teachers.

L. I think athletes are demonstrating some pretty ineffective ways of staying in the flow. In fact, it seems as if they go in and out of the flow so often that it is difficult to see them in the flow. How can we learn from them?

G. Oh, you learn. You learn how to stay stuck. You learn how to stay in confusion, annoyance, and anger. You learn how to make life more difficult for yourself. You learn disrespect, disbelief, anger, doubt, boredom, judgment, frustration, impatience, cowardice, lack of discipline, confusion, denial, and fear. All inner tools. You have learned these very well. Sport has been a great teacher.

L. I wouldn't call that great!

G. Have you not learned well?

L. Well, yes! But great it's not!

G. You only say that because you judge these tools to be less than other tools you have.

L. Well, aren't they? Isn't belief better than mistrust?

G. Why would one be better than another? They are merely tools. As I've told you before, when you use a tool for the purpose it was meant to be used, it is efficient. All the tools I have given you are meant to help you. They all have value. It is in the misuse of them that you find problems. That is why we are writing this book. That is why I am telling you in clear and simple terms how to use them. It is up to you to heed my instructions. I do not insist. You can use anger in any way you choose. I am merely telling you how the tool works so that you can choose the one that is appropriate for your intention.

L. Why do we even need to be told how they work? It seems so obvious the way you explain them. Why don't we just know that?

G. You do! That's why you say they are so obvious. They are.

L. So why do we just as obviously choose the wrong tool?

G. By example! You imitate what you see and hear! This is all fine and good. For it does not matter which path home you decide to travel. You will arrive. Of that you can be sure. Has that not always been my promise?

L. Has it?

G. Yes, of course.

L. When did you promise that? How do we know of this promise?

G. It is in the deepest part of your being. Do you really think you could live in a physical body if living in a physical body was all there was to life? You would have quit a long time ago. There would have been no purpose. No reason for it. No hope.

L. I see what you mean. But not everyone believes that.

G. They do not use hope. As you would say, they have lost hope. You do not have to believe in me, consciously, to have hope. You have free will. You can believe in anything you want to. Still, you all have the same inner tools at your disposal.

Hope is merely one of your tools. If you decide not to use it, that is your choice.

L. Doesn't it bother you that some people don't even believe in you? They think that when they die, that's it.

G. No. That is their choice. A choice is not much of a choice, if you have to choose one and will be punished for choosing the other. But as I have said, each tool has a purpose, a function. If you choose to use a certain tool, you will feel the effects of the tool. It will always work as it's meant to. Of this you can be sure. You can choose a tool that is not appropriate for what you would like to accomplish. Your athlete chose fear and impatience in her match. They worked very well.

L. What do you mean, they worked very well? She couldn't play her game at all!

G. I said the tools worked very well. What is the purpose of fear? Fear blocks your energy or scatters it, depending on the form of fear you choose. She chose fear in the form of doubt and disbelief. Was her energy not blocked?

L. Yes, but . . .

G. But what? You cannot have it both ways!

If you choose a certain tool, all it can do is what it knows how to do, what it is meant to do.

Doubt cannot inspire you. Doubt cannot move you. What did I tell you about doubt?

L. You said that doubt was meant to block us from doing something. It gives us a chance to study the situation, perhaps, or get more information or look at other choices.

G. Yes, very good. You listen well!

L. Thank you. You make me smile! It feels so good when you are pleased with me.

G. And you think I am not pleased with you at times?

L. Aren't you displeased with me at times?

G. And when would those times be?

L. Well, probably when I am angry and impatient.

G. Are these not tools I have given you?

L. Yes, but . . .

G. But at times you misuse them. You make a choice that is not clear with your intention. But then isn't it your intention that is unclear? All of your tools are meant to help you. They are all meant to be used. It is your lack of awareness, naturally, of the function of the tool that causes, the undesired result. Not the tool. The tool does only as it can do. You are the one with free will, not the tools. Tools are only tools. You choose the tools. That is all. Powerful as they may be. If your intention is to clean the carpet, certainly you would not use a hammer instead of a vacuum? Well, perhaps you would! But you can imagine the results, can you not?

L. Yes, I see what you mean. I have a question that may be a little bit off the subject.

G. The subject is always the same. What is your question?

L. Haven't you said that life is not a school because we know everything. That life is a remembering. At least that is what I think you said. It is what I heard, anyway. It seems to me life is a school. We are learning all the time.

G. You are a teacher, Linda. Life will always be a school to you. There is a saying, "A hammer sees everything as a nail." A teacher sees everything as a lesson. What do you think is the essence of what I said?

L. About life being a remembering?

G. Yes, of course. Is that not what we are discussing?

L. Yes, of course. I just seem to have a lot of questions all of a sudden. I can't type them fast enough.

G. Getting impatient, are you?

L. Who me? No, of course not!

G. Back to the question. What is the essence of what I am saying about life?

L. That life is the process of us recreating who we are.

G. And how can you recreate who you are if you don't know who you are?

L. I can't. Go on, please.

G. Life is the process of recreating who you are, and you can't recreate who you are if you didn't know who you are.

L. I got a little bit lost there. Let me see if I have it straight. We are recreating who we are because we are not who we are until we do?

G. Very good! You have it!

L. How can we not be who we are?

G. You can't. You are always you, of course. But whether you are the highest form of you is another question. You are unlimited in who you are.

When you choose a more limited form of who you are, that form is perhaps less of you, but it is you nonetheless.

L. Now I do get it! In each choice we make, we are manifesting in form, who we are. If it feels right, we stay with the choice. We are always choosing, always discovering, more of who we are. We are unlimited in who we are. Therefore we can choose to be limited as well as unlimited. All is a creation of who we are.

G. Yes!

L. Are we ever able to complete the creation?

G. How can you complete unlimited creation?

L. So we never know totally who we are?

G. Here is the difference. You can remember who you are in moments of hope and inspiration. Aren't these moments incredible?

L. Oh, yes, they are!

G. You do this often with your clients. You guide them to this place of knowing. You are a good guide, Linda. Even in your role as a teacher, don't you often say you are teaching them something they already know? That you are merely helping them to remember?

L. Yes, I do. It feels like that. Even when they say they didn't know it, I still feel as if I am reminding them of something they have merely forgotten.

G. Yes, that is what you are doing. And what is it that they are remembering?

L. That they are love.

G. Yes. That is all you need to remember. You are love.

L. Love!

G. Yes, wonderful, isn't it?

L. Yes! You have me smiling again. I was getting so serious about this teaching and recreation thing.

G. Love will do that to you. Makes you smile! Love is light. Turns the corners of your mouth upward, it's so light!!! Linda, you are teaching. Be not confused about what you are doing. You know what you are doing. Teaching is natural for you. It is the role you have chosen. To deny that would be to deny a part of yourself.

You are doing this by teaching the uses of each of the inner tools. You are teaching people how the body system is meant to function at its basic level. And you are teaching them how to access these tools. At the deepest level, you all know who you are. Of course you do. But you are in a physical body now. When you can remember in each situation, in each moment of your life that you are love, you will come from love in each and every situation in your life. Then you will know how to use your inner tools as they are meant to be used. With love. From a place of love. In love. And you, Linda, will be out of a job!

L. Oh dear! What will I do then?

G. Never fear! When that day comes, you will know what to do!

L. Are you saying it's a long way off? I must not be a very good teacher.

G. Wow! How did you jump to that conclusion?

L. If it is going to take such a long time for people to learn how to use their inner tools and how to remember who they are, I must not be doing a very good job of teaching them.

G. Interesting how you take on other people's responsibility. No, Linda. You are an excellent teacher. If you didn't know that, you wouldn't be teaching. And you certainly wouldn't be writing this book. What were you telling Chanda about friendship?

L. Friendship? Oh, yes! She was asking me about a situation in her life. She is soul-searching. She comes up with questions that move me to search even further for answers. She was not feeling good about her relationship with some of the athletes on the tennis team. Her intention was to be better friends with them.

G. What did you tell her?

L. I told her that it was up to her to be a friend. To be the kind of friend she wanted to be. And that it wasn't up to the other women to determine the kind of friend she was. If they decided not to be good friends, that was their choice. She could still choose to be a good friend to them. I told her that it is always about her. The choices she makes.

G. And what if the other women choose not to be good friends with her.

L. Then she can choose other people as her friends. And maybe she wasn't meant to be good friends with all the team members right now. Maybe, they have other things to do. But in no way does this have to determine for her how she lives her life. That is up to her.

G. It is hard for young people, all thrown together because of a common interest, to understand that they may have different interests in other areas. Acceptance is the tool she is learning to use—not an easy one to learn at such a young age.

L. Why is that? What difference does age make? I would think it to be easier at a younger age.

G. Easier in the sense that perhaps youth does not have as much experience to accept. Less to accept gets confused with easier to accept.

L. And so they have less practice?

G. Yes. The more you practice acceptance, the easier it gets. Now, if you have lived more years, but in those years you have not practiced acceptance, it is harder for you. But only because you will have to learn how to accept before you can accept. What is Chanda learning?

L. She is learning how to be herself.

G. Does she know who she is?

L. Consciously? Not all of the time.

G. Make no mistake of it, she knows who she is. She is choosing to learn about tools that you may consider negative. Negative is merely negative. It creates a response, just as positive does. It does not mean she doesn't know at her core who she is. She demonstrated it beautifully last summer when her boyfriend had a stroke. She came from her essence then. And love healed.

L. When she told me about the things she did, I got chills. She was such a beautiful expression of love.

G. She was a beautiful expression of herself!

Highlights

1. Acknowledge what is bothering you, so you can't hide in "I don't know" or denial.
2. Confusion and denial are your body's way of giving you time to accept what is going on, to find another way, to find an answer, or to prepare yourself for the next step.
3. There always comes a time to move on, to continue in the flow of life's energy.
4. Unawareness of the natural flow of life's energy causes anger and frustration in the body—this may be a sign that it is time to move on.
5. Allow your experiences to be a part of the fabric of your life.
6. I am telling you how these tools are meant to be used. You must choose the correct one.
7. You do not have to believe in me to have hope.
8. Hope is merely one of your tools.
9. Your tools always work. If you choose frustration, you will be frustrated.
10. The tool can only do what it is meant to do. Doubt cannot inspire you. Doubt cannot move you.
11. Life is the process of recreating who you are.
12. In each choice you make, you manifest who you are.
13. When you choose a more limited form of who you are, that form is perhaps less of you, but it is you nonetheless.
14. Fear is merely fear. It creates a response, just as does love.

23

Preparing for

Higher-level Performance

G. Your life in a body will be much easier when you understand that all you can ever do is do what feels right to you. If you make choices based on someone else's opinion, you will be living someone else's life. And I can tell you this, it is very hard to be a better someone else than a better you!

L. Excellent point!

G. Is there anything else you would like to know? You are asking the questions, after all!

L. Well, I'm not sure whether we have explained everything about how we can prepare the body before an important event or situation in our lives so that we can perform at higher and higher levels.

G. Okay. Fair enough. Let's stay with the sport example. You'll easily see that it could apply to anything going on in your life. So, what do you do with athletes?

L. All right. I sit them down and tell them they need to decide how they are going to play the next day. I have them tell me what they are going to do physically, mentally, emotionally, and spiritually. I want them to have a clear intention. I want them to communicate clearly with their bodies about what they want their bodies to do.

G. Good. Now, give an example of how you do this. Be more specific. Let's say you are talking to Martina.

L. Okay! I'll pretend I am talking to her, now.

"Martina, what are you going to do physically, tomorrow, in your match?"

"I'm going to keep my feet moving, breathe, and track the ball with my eyes," she responds.

"Good! You want to keep it simple. Stay with the basics. If you do the basics, your body will follow with your strengths. It is the fundamentals that break down first. Your powerful forehand falls apart only after the feet stop moving, the eyes stop tracking the ball, or the breathing stops," I instruct.

G. So how does Martina let her body know that this is what she wants it to do?

L. She talks to her body. Her feet, her eyes, and her breath. And she uses visualization, too. This seems the most direct route to the body.

G. You are right. The simpler you are, the clearer you are. Go on, what next?

L. I ask, "Martina, what are you going to do mentally?"

"After every point I am going to direct my body with positive instruction. If I hit a good shot, I'll say something like 'good job,' to anchor in the shot. If I lose the point by missing the shot, I'll say something like, 'That's okay,' to let my body know that I am still with it. That I believe in it. That I haven't deserted it, just because I missed the point. Then I make the correction. Something like, 'Next time just hit it more out in front of you,' or 'Next time, just run faster.' That sort of thing. Simple corrections. The body knows what to do with them. I stay with the basics. That way the mind won't get in the way. It won't have a chance to go off on a tangent," responds Martina.

G. This is an important part of the process. The mind needs guidance, or it will go all over the place. Your thoughts determine the emotions you choose to use to fuel your body to higher and higher levels of performance. If your thoughts are lower-level thoughts, your performance will be a lower-level performance. Choose only the thoughts that will help you. If a thought doesn't serve you, let it go, and choose one that does.

Be aware of the thoughts that you put into words.

Thoughts spoken have even more influence over you. Self-talk is one way that you let your body know what you want it to do. If you want it to play at a high level, you have to guide it there. Tearing yourself down will not raise your level of performance. Your body always listens to the signals you give it. If you want to play consistently at a high level, you must be consistent with what you are telling your body to do. Mixed messages lead to mixed performance. Then what do you do?

L. Then I ask Martina to tell me which inner tools she is going to use.

G. Why is that important?

L. Because otherwise she may not be prepared for situations in which she will need them. And she may choose inappropriate tools in the heat of the moment.

G. Wonderful! Good plan! Keep going.

L. Okay.

> "Martina, tell me at least three tools that you are going to need tomorrow in your match."
>
> "Patience, confidence and joy."
>
> "Good. When do you need patience?"
>
> "When I start to get impatient."
>
> "Yes, the sooner you are aware of your impatience, the easier it is to move back into patience. How will you know that you have moved into impatience?"
>
> "I usually start rushing my shots. I don't do my between points routine. I feel like I have to win NOW!"

G. What does she do to move out of impatience?

L. She takes a deep breath and repeats silently something like, "I'm okay. I'm safe. I am in the right place at the right time, doing and saying the right thing." By turning her focus to her breathing, she centers herself and is able to smooth out her energy and get back in the natural flow.

G. And what about confidence. When does she need that?

L. All the time. I tell her that if she feels herself moving into doubt or, from an energy standpoint, blocked, then it's time to choose confidence, again.

G. How does she generate confidence?

L. With her breath, her body movements, and her thoughts. She centers herself with her breathing. She moves with bold, strong, outward-flowing movements. Mentally, she tells herself that she is choosing confidence—with self-talk such as, "I am strong. I am confident. I love this game. Just keep your feet moving," statements like that. If she needs more help moving into confidence, she visualizes herself feeling confident and imitates her visualization.

G. How quickly is she able to change from doubt to confidence?

L. The more she practices and trains, the faster she's able to do it. Right now, it still takes her awhile. Sometimes a few games, even.

G. As long as she guides her mind to thoughts that she is strong and confident, she won't have room for thoughts that keep her in doubt.

L. Why does it take so long sometimes?

G. It doesn't take very long once she does the process. It is the decision to choose confidence that takes time. Once you choose confidence, you can move from doubt to confidence in a flash. She may still lose points, of course. You know it is impossible to guarantee the winning of points in a tennis match, and impossible to guarantee the winning of an account in a business deal. But you can guarantee that Martina will have the best chance of winning if she plays with confidence. It's nearly impossible to win with doubt. But since there is another body involved, she may win because the other person loses. Confidence keeps your energy flowing. Doubt blocks your energy.

L. That makes it pretty clear why doubt doesn't work in that situation! Why do athletes have so much trouble understanding that?

G. Because they allow their heads to get in the way. Remember, your mental body can think anything. And it will, if you don't guide it. During competition or when you are doing many things, you want to be sure your heart is involved. Choosing the most efficient emotions for what you want to achieve is part of the game. It separates the higher-level athlete from the lower-level ones, the successful from the unsuccessful. Emotion is what fuels your body. You certainly don't want to put in the wrong fuel, now do you? You wouldn't pour gasoline down your throat, would you? Not the right physical fuel! It's just as important to choose the correct emotional fuel to reach your goal.

L.   Why is it so important to decide ahead of time which emotions you are going to use?

G.   Emotions are tools. You need to know which tools you are going to use. Preparation. If you have moved into doubt, it can be pretty tough to know what to choose that will get you out of it. Inherent in doubt is doubt, you know!! But if you have planned ahead, all you have to do is look for the signals that tell you to go to your plan.

L.   What signals?

G.   You will feel uncomfortable. You will not be playing well. You will feel that your shots are just a little off. Or, if you don't recognize it right away, a lot off!

L.   What about joy? How does she draw out joy?

G.   That is really quite easy. She reminds herself how much she enjoys playing. How much she loves the game. How great it is to be playing. "This is fun," she says to herself. She tunes into positive energy. She takes deep breaths after every point. She smiles to herself when a point is well played—whether she wins the point or not. She walks with a lift in her step. Her eyes are dancing.

L.   What if her energy is still blocked or scattered?

G.   It won't be. If it is, she is not doing what I have said to do. Now, she may still be losing. That's another question. What if she needs to change something because she is still losing? Let's say that confidence, patience, and joy aren't enough. She may need determination if the points are going back and forth. Winning a game, then losing, then winning, then losing and so on. Usually, when both players are using confidence, and the match is up in the air, the one who is most determined wins.

L. So depending on the situation, the athlete who is able to use most efficiently her inner tools will come out ahead?

G. Yes. Assuming the level of competence is similar. Emotions make up the different flavors of life. You are meant to express emotions in your body. Doing so is one of the greatest joys of being in a body.

L. It's pretty simple when we just follow the needs and functions of our bodies. What about the spiritual body?

G. Yes, what about it? Let's get back to Martina. What do you tell her to do to prepare her spiritual body?

L. I tell her to remind herself of her mission. Why she plays. She reads over the mission statement she wrote earlier.

G. Very good. The spirit is the driving force. It is what keeps you going. Knowing why you are playing before you play will help you to stay strong and on purpose. Your intent will remain clear when your spirit is involved.

L. What happens if she loses spirit?

G. All she has to do is remind herself why she is playing. The spirit will be there. If she has been nourishing her spirit with inspiration before and after her matches, her spirit will be strong and supportive. As will it be in life!

L. As in life. Sport is a reflection of everyday life.

If your energy is blocked, unblock it. If it is scattered, gather it. And if it is flowing, go with the flow.

G. Once you understand these basic instructions you can go to the next level.

L. The next level? That sounds intriguing. We haven't talked about anything all that spiritual, have we?

G. Oh, yes, we have, my child. All of life is a spiritual experience. The physical experience is a small part in comparison. So once you have learned how your body functions most efficiently, you can turn yourself more easily toward your soul purpose.

L. I like that idea. So many of these things seem to take up time that I'd rather use doing something else.

G. Yet you have chosen to inhabit a body. Practice the instructions in this book over and over again until you are highly skilled at living in a body. Each time you read something you will discover a meaning you didn't see the time before. Experience the body as the magnificent vehicle it is! As long as you are in your body, you will learn about yourself through your body. Therefore, love your body. It is your ride home.

L. It feels as if we are nearing the end. What do you suggest we do now?

G. Do you have any more questions?

L. Not at the moment. Now I am excited! We must be near the end.

G. Of this book. Yes! But there is more . . .

Index

Index

Index

For information on seminars and speeches, call Linda LeClaire at 612-448-2305 or e-mail LJLeClaire@aol.com. For additional copies of this book or selections from Linda LeClaire's series of mental training audiotapes, use this form:

Name_____

Address_____

City/State/Zip_____

Daytime Phone_____

Audiotape	Qty	Price	Total
The Confidence Factor	_____	$12.95	_____
Tennis/Singles Play	_____	$12.95	_____
Basketball	_____	$12.95	_____
Baseball	_____	$12.95	_____
Golf	_____	$12.95	_____

With Dr. Bryce Young:

	Qty	Price	Total
Quantum Doubles	_____	$12.95	_____
From Anger to Athletic Excellence	_____	$12.95	_____
Play • Recover • Prepare	_____	$12.95	_____

Book

	Qty	Price	Total
Yes, God Speaks to Women, Too!	_____	$16.95	_____
		Subtotal	_____
	(MN residents) 6.5% sales tax		_____
		*Shipping	_____
		TOTAL	_____

Please send orders with checks payable to:

Linda LeClaire

112256 Eitel Circle

Chaska, MN 55318

*Shipping/handling: Add $3.00 for first tape and $1.00 for each additional tape. Add $4.00 for each book and $2.00 for each additional book. Call or e-mail for orders of more than a dozen and for international shipping rates.